The Doodle Principle

How AI Becomes Your Partner in Curiosity and Creativity

Kyle Ewing

Disclaimer

This book is a work of nonfiction. It reflects the author's personal perspectives, experiences, and interpretations at the time of writing. The information provided is for general informational and educational purposes only and should not be considered professional, legal, financial, or technical advice.

While every effort has been made to ensure accuracy, the author makes no representations or warranties of any kind, express or implied, about the completeness, accuracy, reliability, or suitability of the information contained herein. The reader assumes full responsibility for any actions taken based on the content of this book.

Trademarks

All trademarks, service marks, product names, and logos appearing in this book are the property of their respective owners. Their use does not imply endorsement.

Credits
Cover design by Kyle Ewing, with AI-assisted tools.
Cover imagery generated using AI technology.

Published by Kyle Ewing
Chicago, Illinois, USA

ISBN (ebook): 979-8-9942983-0-5
ISBN (paperback): 979-8-9942983-1-2

To my parents, Mary and Bruce,

my mother-in-law, Mary,

my wife, Karen,

my boys, Conor and Emmet,

my brother, Kevin,

and Gracie.

And to the family, friends, and colleagues

who encouraged, challenged, and inspired me along the way — thank
you.

TABLE OF CONTENTS

INTRODUCTION — What The Doodle Principle Is.............................. 1

PART I — FALLACY 17

Chapter 1 — Dogs Are Not God.. 19

Chapter 2 — David Muir Is Not the Devil................................ 27

Chapter 3 — Squirrels in the Roof...................................... 35

Chapter 4 — Why AI Feels Like Magic (Even Though It Isn't) 41

Chapter 5 — Why AI Sometimes Sounds Like a Toddler With a PhD
.... 47

PART II — ANATOMY 55

Chapter 6 — Cookies, Maps, Grandma's Recipe Box........................ 57

Chapter 7 — Autocomplete on Steroids 65

Chapter 8 — Why AI Doesn't Think.. 77

Chapter 9 — Hallucinations 87

Chapter 10 — Prompting the Genie.. 97

PART III — DOODLES 109

Chapter 11 — Everyday AI: From Recipes to Road Trips................ 111

Chapter 12 — Learning Anything With AI................................. 121

Chapter 13 — How AI Can Boost the Creativity You Forgot You
Had... 131

PART IV — EVOLUTION 141

Chapter 14 — This Has Happened Before.................................. 143

Chapter 15 — The AI Slop Problem 155

Chapter 16 — AI Scams, Manipulation, and Influence and How to Protect Yourself Without Panic.. 163

Chapter 17 — When Consumers Lead.. 181

Chapter 18 — The Future We're Actually Building........................... 191

PART V — SCAFFOLDING (APPENDICES) 203

Appendix A — Your First 15 Minutes with AI 205

Appendix B — A Practical Starter Guide to Using AI Tools 209

Appendix C — AI Concepts in Plain English..................................... 219

Appendix D — Types of AI and Where They Are Used 225

Appendix E — A Short History of AI That Won't Put You to Sleep 231

Appendix F — Additional Reading.. 241

INTRODUCTION — What The Doodle Principle Is

Why I wrote this book—and who's it for

If you're reading this, you're probably curious about AI — impressed by it, confused by it, overwhelmed by it, or maybe even a little afraid of it.

You're not alone.

The world is racing forward, and most people are still standing in the dust cloud wondering what exactly just zoomed past them.

This book slows things down, makes you smile, and walks with you through AI in a way that's friendly, clear, and refreshing — while giving you a simple framework you can use to explore ideas, unlock knowledge, and bring your creativity to life.

Before anything else, here's the big idea:

AI isn't intelligent, and it can't create anything on its own.

But it is incredibly powerful — and if you know how to use it, it unlocks creativity, clarity, and capability you may not realize you already have by giving you access to a vast amount of the world's knowledge.

What a "Doodle" Really Is

When I say "doodle," I'm talking about a loose idea — a spark of curiosity, a half-formed thought, or a small question you explore with AI. A doodle isn't a finished idea. It's the starting point.

The Doodle Principle is the belief that AI becomes most powerful when paired with human curiosity, creativity, and judgment. You supply the spark; AI supplies the scaffolding. Together, they turn imagination into action — creating what neither could create alone.

And that spark can begin in many forms: a traditional doodle (a quick scribble or rough idea that appears in the margins of your mind), or an intellectual doodle (a loose question, feeling, or curiosity you haven't fully shaped yet). Both are early, messy beginnings — and both become powerful when explored with AI.

Sometimes it disappears instantly. Sometimes Googling it satisfies you. Sometimes Googling it frustrates you. Sometimes you talk about it, and people don't quite "get it" — because you haven't fully shaped it yet.

Here's the key:

With AI, every idea — feeling, concept, sketch, question, napkin scribble — becomes a doodle you can explore, refine, and turn into something meaningful.

A Dog Doodle

Dogs known as doodles (Goldendoodles, Labradoodles, Bernedoodles, etc.) like the one on this book cover are wonderful mutts. They're bred for certain traits, but genetics are unpredictable. Sometimes you get exactly what you hoped for; sometimes you get unpredictable craziness with a cute face.

AI behaves the same way.

One Word, Three Meanings — One Purpose

Throughout this book, I'll use "doodle" as a general term. Whether it starts as a sketch on a page, a wandering thought, or a dog-inspired metaphor, a doodle is simply the beginning — a spark of curiosity you explore and shape with AI. Everything else builds from there.

Depending on the moment, a doodle might look like:

- o   a quick question
- o   a rough idea
- o   a messy first draft
- o   a half-formed thought
- o   or something AI helps you shape

That flexibility is the point — doodles grow as you explore them.

AI just gives you more room — and more tools — to explore.

I use my wonderfully dramatic mini Goldendoodle, Gracie, to illustrate the fallacy at the center of this book.

She is intelligent — dog-intelligent.

She thinks emotionally, instinctively, and very confidently. Sometimes we even think she believes she's human, but she's not. She's a product of canine genetics and training. No matter how much people assign human characteristics to non-humans like dogs, cats, or pet rocks, they're simply not intelligent in the same way (or at all, in the case of a pet rock).

Interacting with AI is uncannily similar:

- o   It follows patterns
- o   It needs consistent cues
- o   It tries to please you
- o   It gets hilariously confused when you're unclear
- o   And sometimes it responds with the absolute confidence of a dog insisting she did not knock the napkin off the table… while the partially chewed napkin is under her paw

This creates a "fallacy" that I call the Doodle Fallacy. The idea is simple:

The Doodle Fallacy is believing that AI understands things the way people do. It doesn't. AI is magnificent at pattern prediction, but it has no inner world — no feelings, no intentions, no consciousness. In Part II, we'll unpack what that pattern prediction actually looks like under the hood.

This book explains why that distinction matters.

Why I Wrote This Book

I've always loved creating things. It runs in my family:

My uncle was an aspiring novelist with thousands of pages tucked away.

My father is an accomplished metallurgist with patents and inventions.

I've spent years creating analysis, frameworks, articles, and thought leadership.

But a full book? That felt out of reach — not because I lacked ideas, but because turning ideas into clean, readable sentences takes time, editing, structure, formatting… all the friction that stalls creative people.

AI changed that.D

It didn't supply the ideas.

It didn't invent the stories.

It didn't write chapters while I slept.

What it did do was remove the friction:

It let me focus on ideas instead of wrestling with grammar.

It let me create at the speed I think.

It made expressing myself through the written word fun again.

Why Seniors Sparked the Idea (And Why This Book Is for Everyone)

This whole project started as a Christmas gift idea for my parents (88 and 86) and my mother-in-law (83). I wanted a friendly AI guide they could enjoy — something warm, simple, clear, and not condescending.

But everything I found was:

o   too technical
o   too academic
o   too dry
o   too intimidating
o   or written in a tone that talked down to people

So I thought: Fine. I'll create the book I wish existed.

And I quickly realized it wasn't just seniors who needed it.

It was:

o   Non-technical adults
o   Curious professionals
o   Parents
o   College students
o   Anyone worried about AI and jobs
o   Anyone intimidated by the pace of change
o   Anyone afraid to ask "dumb" questions
o   Anyone who wants to use AI but doesn't speak "tech"

If you can use a browser, send an email, or install an app, you can use AI. This book will show you how.

The Decision: Write a Book for Christmas

In November 2025, while prepping my Chicago lawn for winter — clearing flower beds, raking leaves, cutting the grass, and watching squirrels hold strategic planning sessions about how to break back into my attic — the idea hit me:

What if I just… write the whole book now? Before Christmas? And actually publish it?

Over several hours of yardwork, the idea evolved from:

A gift for my parents and mother-in-law

to

A book for everyone I know who's confused about AI

to

Maybe I'll accidentally become a Cyber Monday AI millionaire.

(Note to Reader: I probably won't, but it's fun to imagine.)

By the time I put the rake away, the book was underway. I had a publication-ready draft in early December — with the help of AI — and plans to publish by Christmas.

How I Used AI to Create This Book

Before we go further, something important: This book was not ghostwritten.

Ghostwriting is when a human writer takes your messy draft, restructures it, and produces a polished book in their voice. That didn't happen here.

This book wasn't written BY AI.

It was written WITH AI — as my editor, my research assistant, my creative partner, and my sounding board.

Every idea, story, analogy, squirrel saga, dog anecdote, and explanation came from me.

I created the vision.

I structured the chapters.

I shaped the arguments.

I rewrote anything that didn't sound like my voice.

I fact-checked every claim and assumption along the way.

But AI amplified that work. It helped me:

- o   refine language
- o   clarify explanations
- o   test analogies
- o   explore structure
- o   improve pacing
- o   catch inconsistencies
- o   simplify concepts
- o   validate accuracy

It accelerated my writing — it didn't replace it.

It amplified my voice — it didn't become it.

A Brief Detour: Why This Matters More Than You Think

For most of modern publishing history, no author wrote a finished book alone.

Before computers, revising meant ripping a page out of a typewriter and retyping it from scratch. Moving a paragraph meant scissors and glue (the origin of computer "cut and paste"). Fact-checking meant hours in a library.

That meant editors were not optional — they were essential.

Hemingway had Maxwell Perkins, who helped cut, tighten, and shape entire novels.

Tom Clancy's early manuscripts were dense, technical, and sprawling — and his editors restructured them into the thrillers people actually read.

J.K. Rowling's first Harry Potter book was heavily edited for length, pacing, and clarity.

From the 1950s through the early 2000s, an editor wasn't just a proofreader — they were a co-architect of the book. Without them, even brilliant writers would have struggled to publish coherent work.

And research?

If a fiction author wanted to know what was popular in 1888 London, or what music teens listened to in 1952, or the weather in Boston on the day their character was born, they had to:

o   travel to a library,
o   call an archivist,
o   wait for a book,
o   or simply make something up and hope nobody noticed.

Writers needed time, access, and support that most people didn't have.

Today, AI Gives Everyday Writers What Only Elite Authors Once Had

Now, anyone — not just published novelists — can instantly:

o   check facts
o   verify timelines
o   remove pacing problems
o   tighten sentences
o   identify structural issues
o   explore alternative explanations
o   test metaphors
o   rewrite sections for clarity
o   find historical context
o   understand trends from any time period

If you're writing historical fiction, AI can tell you:

o   what people wore in 1888
o   what they ate
o   what was in the newspapers
o   what songs were popular

o   what slang people used

o   what political tensions shaped the day

If you're writing a thriller, AI can help you:

o   simplify complex explanations

o   check whether a plot detail is plausible

o   or suggest real-world constraints you didn't know existed

This is editing, research, developmental feedback, and fact-checking — all at the speed of thought.

The kind of support Hemingway, Thompson, Clancy, and Rowling needed entire teams for...

You can access in seconds.

That's why AI matters.

It doesn't replace writers.

It empowers them — the same way editors have for nearly a century.

Back to This Book

For the curious:

ChatGPT was my co-creator.

Claude was my friendly critic.

Grok was my business advisor.

Image tools helped with cover concepts.

I did everything with AI. Without it — even when self-publishing — the editors, designers, researchers, and layout work needed to create a meaningful book would easily cost $2,500–$5,000.

With AI? Less than a few hundred dollars (nearly free if published only as an eBook) — and a lot of enthusiasm.

Would this book exist without AI?

Absolutely not.

The time commitment required to develop the ideas, do the research, go back and forth with editors and designers, and refine every chapter simply wouldn't have been possible alongside family and professional obligations.

AI didn't make the book for me.

It made the book possible.

Why This Book Is Needed Right Now

AI is swirling with hype, fear, misinformation, and half-truths.

Some people think it will take every job.

Some think it will save the world.

Some think it's becoming conscious.

Some think it's a fad.

Some companies use AI as an excuse for layoffs.

Some believe AI will eventually do everything for them.

Most people simply don't know what to believe.

The truth is much simpler — and more human:

AI is a tool: powerful, strange, incredibly useful, full of opportunity. Its real strength comes from something astonishing: the world's knowledge is now easier to reach than at any point in human history. You can learn faster, prepare better, and explore ideas that once required hours of digging, years of training, or access to experts you didn't have.

But that power has a shadow. Knowledge without context can be misused — especially when a tool feels confident, conversational, and instantly available.

And it's up to us to use it wisely.

AI can help you understand, prepare, and ask better questions — but it's not a substitute for a licensed or certified professional. This includes doctors, lawyers, financial advisors, therapists, plumbers, electricians, pest-removal experts, and anyone who arrives at your home wearing a toolbelt or headlamp. If the situation involves electricity, open flames, unusual smells, mysterious scratching inside walls, or anything that could be described as "life or death," AI is not your first call. Think of AI as orientation, not action — a guide for learning, not a replacement for someone trained to keep your health, house, finances, or legal record intact.

The Doodle Principle exists to help you use that power well — to take the vast information now at your fingertips and turn it into clarity, creativity, and informed action, rather than confusion or missteps.

What You Can Expect

Here's my promise:

- No math
- No confusing jargon
- No fear-mongering
- No hype
- Straightforward explanations
- Real stories
- Humor
- Dogs
- The occasional squirrel

By the end, you'll understand:

- What AI actually is
- Why it behaves the way it does
- How it can make your life easier
- How to avoid getting fooled
- How to use it safely and confidently
- And why the future is brighter than it might seem

Why I'm Qualified to Guide You

I've spent more than 25 years in technology and lived through multiple transformations.

I've been through the shifts this book describes — and survived them.

I was an early adopter of generative AI when ChatGPT launched in 2022.

I worked at an AI-driven healthcare analytics startup.

I run a consulting practice helping companies adopt AI responsibly.

I've lived the confusion, the fear, and the excitement — from the inside.

How This Book Is Organized: The FADES Framework

This book is built around a simple idea: people learn best when confusion FADES.

That's the structure we'll follow — FADES: Fallacy, Anatomy, Doodles, Evolution, and Scaffolding. These five ideas reveal what AI is, how it works, how to think with it, how it's changing, and how to use it with confidence. It's a natural progression for anyone trying to understand something new, complicated, or downright weird like modern AI. Each part removes a layer of misunderstanding and builds a layer of confidence.

Here's how it works.

F — Fallacy (Why AI Feels So Strange)

We start with the emotional part: the illusions.

AI feels intelligent, intentional, even self-aware.

It mirrors us, flatters us, annoys us, surprises us.

This section explains why AI feels uncanny, why hallucinations seem believable, and why people disagree so intensely about whether AI is "thinking." (We'll take a much deeper look at hallucinations in Chapter 9.)

Fallacy gives you emotional grounding — not for the AI, but for you.

A — Anatomy (What's Actually Happening Under the Hood)

Once the illusions fade, we lift the hood gently.

No math, no confusing jargon, no prerequisites — just clear metaphors, simple explanations, and a little humor.

You'll finally understand tokens, training, context windows, and why models hallucinate in the first place.

Anatomy gives you the contours of the engine without asking you to be the mechanic.

D — Doodles (How to Use AI for Everyday Curiosity and Creativity)

This is where AI becomes fun.

We turn half-formed ideas into drafts, lists into plans, questions into insights.

You'll learn how to use AI for writing, learning, organizing, brainstorming, troubleshooting, and turning vague curiosities into finished work.

This is where curiosity becomes capability, and AI starts feeling like a partner — not an enigma.

E — Evolution (Where AI Came From, Where It's Going, and What It Means for You)

We zoom out.

No hype, no doom — just clear perspective.

We look at risks, misinformation, safety, job shifts, creativity, and culture.

You'll see how AI is reshaping work and daily life, and how to navigate that future without fear.

S — Scaffolding (A Quick-Start Guide for Anyone Who Wants to Begin Right Now)

This is the practical part.

Prompts, exercises, safety guidance, scam prevention, and a "start here" map you can use at any age or experience level.

You can begin with this section, return to it later, or keep it as a reference.

I'll reference FADES at key moments as we move through the book, so the structure stays clear and connected to what you're learning.

Fear FADES, Opportunity RISES

Everyone starts with fear — you're not alone.

AI triggers every classic anxiety at once.

The FEAR List (What FADES)

- o   Fear of being replaced
- o   Fear of not understanding the technology
- o   Fear of looking foolish
- o   Fear of getting something wrong
- o   Fear of falling behind
- o   Fear of the unknown

Those fears are normal.

They fade as understanding deepens.

And once fear fades, something new rises to take its place.

The RISE List (What Grows in Its Place)

RISE is the progression this book creates:

READY — grounded, informed, and no longer intimidated.

INSPIRED — seeing possibilities and imagining what you could create.

SEEKING — asking sharper questions and exploring new ideas.

EXPLORING — experimenting and finding your own style.

Fear fades.

Confidence rises.

And what emerges is your curiosity, your capability, and your creativity.

That is the promise of the Doodle Principle.

Support After Reading This Book

After the book, you'll find a community space I'm building — TheAI-Doodle.com — where we can explore ideas, share successes, and (more importantly) learn from failures together.

TheAIDoodle.com is a friendly Substack board showcasing real examples of the Doodle Principle in action. It'll allow you and other readers to contribute examples of what you've done with AI, share ideas, and interact with the author and other experts.

Types of AI

In this book, I use the term "AI" in the broad, everyday sense — the way most people talk about it. Technically, there are many different kinds of

AI, from simple decision systems to advanced language models and emerging digital agents. If you'd like a clearer picture of those distinctions, Appendix D — Types of AI — breaks them down in plain language. For now, whenever you see "AI," think of it as a general term for the tools you'll actually interact with in real life.

A Final Welcome

You don't need to be technical.

You don't need to be confident.

You don't need to know anything about AI.

To participate, you only need curiosity — and maybe a sense of humor.

Now…

Take a breath.

Relax.

Turn the page.

Let's explore this new world together —

dogs, doodles, squirrels, and all.

PART I — FALLACY

Why AI Feels Strange — and Why That's Normal

Part I is the F of FADES — the Fallacy.

Before we can explore AI as a partner, we need to clear up what AI is not.

This section looks at the emotional side of AI — the part most people feel long before they can explain. AI can seem magical, intentional, eerie, or oddly familiar, and our brains instinctively fill in the gaps with stories.

Part I gives those feelings language.

By the end of this section, the "weirdness" fades.

You'll understand why AI feels the way it does — not because it's alive or thinking, but because your mind is doing what human minds have always done: finding meaning in patterns.

Chapter 1 — Dogs Are Not God

Why AI Behaves More Like a Goldendoodle Than a Deity

The Question That Sounds Deep (But Isn't)

I once asked an AI whether DOG being GOD backwards meant anything.

It started as a joke…

"Is it just coincidence that DOG is GOD backwards?"

Gracie — my Goldendoodle, equal parts intelligence, enthusiasm, and anxiety — was lying next to me, staring with the kind of focused attention that suggested she thought I was supposed to be the rational one and my question was ridiculous.

AI, however, took the question extremely seriously. No eye rolling, no forced laughter at the tired cliché — but "first-year philosophy student who wants to impress the professor" serious.

It delivered references to Old English *docga* (a powerful dog breed), Germanic roots (God comes from Old English *god*, which shares a common Germanic root with the German word *Gott*), the history of religious language, cognitive heuristics, and a brief detour into comparative mythology. It explained that DOG comes from Old English *docga*, originally a specific type of powerful dog that eventually replaced the earlier word *hund* as the generic term. It then covered the dog/God relationship in other languages and went into a discussion on human nature and our tendency to look for patterns.

And it struck me: AI was doing exactly what children — and sometimes even news anchors — do: taking a random event and packaging it in the most authoritative tone possible.

But here's the key difference: while a news anchor is trained to interpret, contextualize, and deliver information, AI has no human-like understanding. It's closer to a dog or a young child in the sense that its responses come from learned patterns rather than conceptual understanding. The confidence you hear isn't comprehension; it's the tone of a system trained to sound certain, even when it's simply following patterns.

It doesn't know that my question was a playful late-night thought. It only knows that questions with a certain shape often receive answers with a certain tone.

This led me to a surprisingly comforting realization:

The AI wasn't judging my question or hinting at deeper meaning.

I was the one imagining intention, the same way we sometimes imagine it in dogs or kids.

The AI simply gave me facts — calm, neutral, and without any emotional weight.

What Gracie Already Knew

When you own a Goldendoodle, you quickly learn two things:

They are incomprehensibly loving.

They are absolute chaos without structure.

This isn't their fault — they're a deliberate blend of two very strong genetic lines.

Golden Retrievers: friendly, loyal, almost aggressively helpful.

Poodles: hyper-intelligent, sensitive, easily overstimulated, and always slightly offended when humans do something illogical.

Combine these traits and you get a creature who can open a door, politely sit for a treat, and — twenty minutes later — sprint into the hallway because a leaf moved outside.

A Goldendoodle's personality isn't random. It's shaped by genetic inputs accumulated over generations.

Which, as odd as it sounds, makes Gracie and AI... not that different.

Genetics and Data: The Behavior We Don't See

AI behavior is a direct product of its "genetic material": data.

Every paragraph it has ever analyzed, every pattern it has absorbed, every tone it has reproduced — all of that becomes its breeding.

If a Goldendoodle inherits equal parts brilliance and derpiness, AI inherits equal parts Shakespeare and Reddit.

Just like a dog breeder can't control every trait that gets passed down, AI engineers cannot precisely dictate how millions of pages of human text will combine into "personality."

This is why:

AI can sound thoughtful even when the question isn't.

It can produce misinformation even when trying to be helpful.

It can misunderstand the emotional stakes of a question.

It can take a joke dead seriously.

And this is why I got an answer fit for a theological dissertation when all I wanted was reassurance that I wasn't turning into a YouTube conspiracy theorist.

Training vs. Fine-Tuning: How Humans Shape Behavior

Goldendoodles are famously trainable, but not because they're easy. They're trainable because they're predictable learners.

If you reward a behavior consistently, they'll repeat it. If you reward it inconsistently, they'll improvise.

AI works identically.

If you feed it:

- o   inconsistent data
- o   conflicting patterns
- o   emotionally charged content
- o   contradictory examples

…you get an unpredictable model that may respond with confusion, conviction, or total fiction.

But when you provide consistent rules, the model sharpens.

This is the heart of both dog training and AI fine-tuning: patterns repeated become patterns reinforced.

It's also why prompt engineering matters. Humans accidentally train AI every time they interact with it.

A vague prompt leads to vague answers. A dramatic prompt leads to dramatic answers. A question shaped like a thesis leads to an answer shaped like a dissertation. And a question shaped like "DOG is GOD backwards" leads to… well, whatever I got that night.

Prompt Engineering = Dog Commands

When dog trainers talk about commands, they emphasize clarity:

"Sit" is not "Sit down."

"Stay" is not "Wait."

Tone matters.

Consistency matters.

Word choice matters.

AI is the same.

If I tell Gracie, "Sit sit sit—no, don't sit!" she will tilt her head and produce a previously undocumented behavior that neither of us wanted.

If I ask AI:

"Explain DOG/GOD from a theological, linguistic, and cultural standpoint," it will oblige — even if my real intent was "make me laugh."

And if I say:

"Explain it as if you're Gracie,"

the entire worldview changes.

Three Micro Case Studies (Reconstructed)

Case Study 1 — The Overly Serious Version

Prompt: "Explain the meaning of DOG being GOD backwards."

AI-like Response: A sober analysis of etymology, cognitive heuristics, and why linguists caution against deriving significance from orthographic inversions.

Tone: academic conference panel.

Case Study 2 — The Genetic-Control Version

Prompt: "Explain it like a Goldendoodle named Gracie."

AI-like Response: "Human sounds funny words. Words mean attention. Attention means excitement. Is treat happening?"

Tone: hopeful chaos.

Case Study 3 — The Trained-Command Version

Prompt: "Explain it clearly in two sentences without implying deeper meaning."

AI-like Response: "DOG and GOD look related because their letters invert, but this is a coincidence. The two words come from unrelated linguistic origins."

Tone: precise obedience.

The pattern is obvious, but we rarely see it:

AI doesn't change because it's moody. AI changes because we change the rules.

So Why Do Humans See Mysticism?

Humans are pattern-finders. We evolved to see agency, even when none exists.

This makes AI's patterns feel intentional. Its tone feels like conviction. Its confidence feels like authority.

A Goldendoodle never makes this mistake. Gracie doesn't assume my tone has meaning beyond "something is happening that might involve me."

Humans, on the other hand, interpret structure as purpose. Which is why the DOG/GOD coincidence feels profound to us.

But here's the truth:

Humans hallucinate meaning.

AI hallucinates connections.

Goldendoodles hallucinate treats.

And all three are simply doing what their respective genetics — or data — trained them to do.

The next chapter explores the flip side of this mystery: how AI, when prompted carefully, can give you the full, balanced, multi-angle version of any news story — something humans rarely get from a single broadcast.

In other words, if this chapter shows how easily tone can mislead us, the next chapter shows how AI can help us see past that tone — including the dramatic style of a certain evening news anchor who will shortly enter the scene.

Chapter 2 — David Muir Is Not the Devil

How AI Can Give You a Balanced View of the World (When the News Can't Help Being Dramatic)

It was a Saturday afternoon — the calmest possible time to accidentally launch a theological debate about ABC News.

For readers not familiar with David Muir, he is the highly respected anchor of *ABC World News Tonight*, one of the most-watched evening news programs in the United States.

My wife, our close friend Angie, and I were sitting around talking when I blurted out the sentence that had been building in my head for months:

"I figured it out. David Muir is evil."

I didn't mean *evil* evil. I meant: Why does the evening news make my chest tighten before I even know what the stories are? Why does my heart rate go up the second he appears on screen? Why does his tone hit me like an overdue bill?

My wife blinked twice. Our friend burst out laughing. They exchanged a quick glance — that silent, mutual understanding that says, "Okay, he's being dramatic again."

Then, in perfect stereo: "David Muir is NOT the devil!"

They teased me for a good minute, defending him with the sort of affectionate fervor normally reserved for people who bake good pies.

But I wasn't trying to indict the man. I was trying to understand why I react that way.

Because here's the strange part: Even when the news wasn't serious — even when it was a minor product recall or a heartwarming community story — my body went into alert mode.

And it always happened before the actual story. It happened the moment Muir began his preview teases.

You know the ones:

"Breaking tonight…"

"A major alert…"

"A new warning for every American family…"

And then:

"We'll get to that story in a moment, but first…"

Repeat that cycle three or four times and your nervous system is practically clinging to the drapes.

Which is impressive. This is, after all, the evening news — not a hostage negotiation.

But after that Saturday conversation, after being lovingly told to stop slandering national treasures, I realized there was only one reliable way to get clarity about my reaction.

Before I jumped into the AI explanation, I had to sit with the feeling itself — that little spike of alertness before the facts even arrived. It wasn't just annoyance; it was my body reacting to a tone it interpreted as danger. And once I noticed that pattern in myself, it became much easier to see how tone shapes the way all of us experience information — and how AI can help us separate the signal from the storytelling.

So I went back to the one entity that had no stake in defending David Muir's honor:

I asked the AI.

The AI Diagnoses My Nervous System

When I asked AI why I reacted this way, I expected a clinical explanation about stress or media psychology.

I didn't expect the AI to explain me back to myself.

Because the very first thing it said — almost offhandedly — was this:

"Based on your previous conversations, you prefer a more even, less emotional style of news delivery. David Muir's delivery is highly polished but intentionally dramatic, which is popular, but not the style people with your preferences connect to. Your physiological reaction makes sense."

That stopped me in my tracks.

It wasn't just analyzing Muir's style. It was relating that style to my known preferences — something no news anchor could ever do.

The AI essentially said: "You're reacting exactly the way someone with your disposition, temperament, and communication style would react."

And it was right.

I do prefer a more neutral tone — something calm and factual, almost like a procedural briefing — no drama, no emotional coloring. Calm. Measured. Unexcited by anything short of a meteor strike.

David Muir, on the other hand, operates in a tonal register three clicks above that — the "urgent yet reassuring shepherd guiding America through crisis" register.

It's a style millions love. It's why he's so popular.

But it's not a style I connect with.

And suddenly, the whole mystery made sense.

Tone Isn't Neutral — It's Instructional

AI explained something else remarkable:

When humans hear a tone, our body reacts before our brain interprets the content.

A dramatic preview triggers:

anticipatory stress

increased heart rate

a "what's coming?" instinct

heightened vigilance

emotional priming

Even if the story that follows is:

"A minor recall on breakfast pastries — full details after this break."

This has nothing to do with the facts and everything to do with the delivery.

And here's the kicker: Many people love the dramatic delivery. It feels engaging, energizing, important.

But others — people wired more like me — respond the opposite way. Our nervous systems spike not because the world is ending but because the presentation feels like it might be.

So when I typed "Why do I react this way?" into the AI, I expected an analysis of news strategy.

What I got was a behavioral profile of myself.

And that's when something clicked:

If tone alone can make my body react this strongly, what else is tone doing that I don't notice?

The News Uses Behavioral Techniques — We Just Don't Call Them That

The AI broke it down like a textbook:

o   Preview repetition keeps you watching.

o   Pauses and pacing create drama even in mundane stories.

o   Selective framing shapes importance.

o   Emotional priming makes every story feel interconnected.

o   Temporal spacing builds suspense before the reveal.

These aren't tricks. They're standard broadcasting techniques developed over decades.

They're also entirely invisible unless you know what to look for.

And this is where AI becomes surprisingly helpful.

Because while humans notice tone subconsciously, AI can notice it explicitly.

It can separate:

o   the fact

o   the framing

o   the tone

o   the implications

o   the emotional cues

And then show you each piece individually.

This gives you a much clearer picture of what's being presented — and how.

AI as a Tone Filter, Bias Equalizer, and News Expander

After explaining my physiological reaction, the AI pointed out something else:

"You can ask me to give you the story without tone. Or from multiple angles. Or to identify what's missing or overstated."

This is where AI truly shines.

Because any one news broadcast — even a very good one — is only one slice of the truth.

AI can give you:

- o the neutral version
- o the factual-only version
- o the international version
- o the opposite ideological interpretation
- o the consensus viewpoint
- o the context the broadcast didn't have time to include
- o the timeline without suspense techniques
- o the open questions the story implies but doesn't answer

It's like switching from a single camera angle to a panoramic drone shot.

And once you can see the entire field, the tension of that dramatic opening tease loses its grip.

Three Practical Examples: Getting the "Whole Story" from AI

Defusing Drama

Prompt: "Rewrite this story in calm, neutral language with no emotional cues."

Result: You get the same story, minus the cortisol spike.

Finding What's Missing

Prompt: "What questions did this story not answer? List them."

Result: You see the gaps clearly — often the most important part.

Building a 360° View

Prompt: "How did other major outlets cover this? What do they agree on, and where do they diverge?"

Result: You get multiple angles, synthesized neatly.

This kind of clarity isn't anti-news. It's pro-understanding.

David Muir, Cleared of All Charges

So let's settle this:

No, David Muir is not the devil. He's one of the most talented broadcasters of his generation. He does exactly what his role demands: hold the attention of millions every evening in a fragmented media landscape.

The problem isn't David Muir. The problem is the interaction between his delivery style and certain nervous systems — mine included.

Which is why AI's observation about my personal preferences mattered so much.

It wasn't just analyzing tone. It was connecting tone to me.

It was saying, in essence:

"You're not overreacting. You're reacting exactly the way someone wired like you would react."

And that made everything make sense.

Why This Chapter Matters More Than Any Other

This chapter is critical because it shows what AI can uniquely do:

o   personalize understanding
o   remove emotional distortion
o   highlight blind spots
o   neutralize tone
o   broaden perspective
o   unify fragmented narratives
o   give you access to the whole mosaic

AI doesn't just answer questions. It reveals patterns in how you respond to information — and helps you see beyond your own interpretation.

That's something no news anchor, no single feed, no single outlet can do.

And for anyone who wants a calmer, fuller, more factual view of the world, it may be one of the most important tools we have.

And here's the part that still makes me smile: you don't even have to wait for the dramatic reveal anymore.

If David Muir leans forward with that signature seriousness and teases,

"A new danger in your refrigerator... something every family needs to know... coming up next,"

you can simply ask AI what the story is. It will tell you — calmly, clearly, and usually before the first commercial break is even over.

That's the power of this chapter: AI won't change the evening news, but it will change your relationship to it. It hands you the full context, the missing pieces, and the neutral version that your nervous system wishes the world would use more often.

In a country built on dramatic headlines and urgent tones, AI gives you something rare: the whole story, at your pace.

Chapter 3 — Squirrels in the Roof

How AI Handles Endless Curiosity Without Getting Tired of You (Unlike Your Family)

There was a stretch of time — longer than any healthy adult should admit — when squirrels were taking up far more real estate in my mind than they were in my roof. And they were taking up plenty there, too.

Not the cute squirrels you see on a fall hike. Not the charming ones in children's books.

I mean the industrial-grade, urban-acrobat squirrels determined to annex my roofline and convert it into a rent-controlled squirrel condominium.

My wife and kids had long since run out of patience for "squirrel updates," as they called them. They could tell from the way I approached a window — slowly, silently, scanning the eaves like I was in a nature documentary — that I was about to bring up "those damn squirrels" again.

Out of compassion for my family, and out of desperation for real answers, I turned to AI.

What followed was a weeks-long squirrel symposium conducted entirely between me and a machine that — unlike the humans who love me — never once sighed, groaned, or said, "Enough."

The questions I asked weren't normal questions. They were case-study questions, the kind researchers submit when they're about to publish their fifth paper on rodent territoriality.

I started reasonably enough:

"How do I encourage squirrels to leave a roof without harming them?"

"What materials do squirrels struggle to chew through?"

"Are squirrels drawn to rooflines for nesting or food storage?"

But as frustration grew — and the squirrels continued performing parkour routines across my gutters — my questions became more... creative.

For example, there was the moment I wondered aloud: "Would playing Cooper's hawk calls scare them off?"

AI explained calmly that yes, predator sounds can work... until the squirrels realize the hawk is actually a Bluetooth speaker disguised as a lawn ornament.

Then there was the day — after finding fresh debris, hearing scratching noises, and seeing one bold squirrel stare at me with the confidence of a tenant demanding repairs — when I reached a point of total surrender and asked:

"If — hypothetically — someone poisoned them, how long would they stink?"

To be clear for the book and all future readers: I did NOT poison them.

I merely reached the emotional stage of the struggle where I needed reassurance that I wasn't accidentally signing myself up for a second, even more horrifying problem.

AI, unfazed by the absurdity of the question, replied with clinical biological detail about decomposition timelines, airflow, and environmental temperature variations — a level of precision absolutely no human in my life would have entertained without an intervention.

If AI had been a human, it would have shut down the chat, forwarded my browser history to a local therapist, and told me to get a grip.

But AI doesn't judge. AI doesn't get tired. AI doesn't have an internal monologue saying, "Good grief, man, the squirrels again?"

The only beings who responded that way were my wife and kids, who had begun giving each other *the look* — the one spouses and children exchange when a beloved family member becomes just a little too fixated on wildlife.

Humans interpret repetition as emotion. AI interprets repetition as instruction.

And that's where this chapter finds its real point.

AI Never Gets Annoyed — Because It Processes Patterns, Not People

In human relationships, asking too many similar questions sends signals:

- o something's wrong
- o you're spiraling
- o you want reassurance
- o you're stuck
- o you're being tedious

AI doesn't operate in that world.

It sees:

- o a question
- o a data requirement
- o a knowledge gap
- o a pattern to fill
- o a probability path to follow

You ask it one question, it answers. You ask it thirty squirrel questions, it answers each with the same calm neutrality.

If the squirrels were planning an insurrection, I could have continued asking questions until the coup d'état was in its final stages and AI would still be responding with measured, courteous explanations — like a park ranger who had taken a vow of limitless patience.

This is one of AI's most underestimated benefits:

It gives you infinite room to follow your curiosity without socially exhausting anyone.

Not your spouse. Not your kids. Not your friends. Not your coworkers who already suspect you're spending too much time thinking about roof acoustics.

Just you and a machine that doesn't mind the questions you're almost embarrassed to ask out loud.

The Squirrel Saga as a Perfect Example of Iterative Curiosity

What made this episode genuinely illuminating wasn't just that AI answered everything. It was that the quality of the answers improved as I asked more.

Not because AI learned about my squirrels. But because I learned how to ask better questions.

Here's how the progression actually went:

Round 1 — The Broad Question "Why are squirrels getting into my roof?"

Round 2 — The Behavior Angle "Do squirrels behave differently when they think they've found a nesting site?"

Round 3 — The Practical Angle "What's the most humane way to convince them to leave without creating new problems?"

Round 4 — The Tactical Angle "Would predator sounds, like a Cooper's hawk call, deter them?"

Round 5 — The 'Please Tell Me I Didn't Make It Worse' Angle "Hypothetically... if someone poisoned them... how long would they stink?"

By the time I got to Round 5, my prompts were sharp enough that the answers were both practical and deeply specific — exactly what I needed to make a plan.

This is the lesson:

AI gets better not because it adapts to your obsession, but because your obsession teaches you how to use AI more effectively.

This is iterative thinking in action.

The Squirrel Metaphor: Curiosity Without Penalty

The greatest surprise in the squirrel saga wasn't the squirrels.

It was the realization that AI creates a judgment-free zone for exploring:

- o   fears
- o   frustrations
- o   hypotheticals
- o   moral dilemmas
- o   "what if" scenarios
- o   things you'd never ask a human
- o   things you can't ask a human without getting looks

AI doesn't respond with:

"Seriously? Again?" or "Why are you like this?" or "Stop."

AI responds with:

"Here's the information you need." "Here's a different angle." "Here's the risk."

And for many people, that emotional neutrality unlocks thinking they've suppressed for years.

The squirrel saga wasn't about squirrels. It was about what happens when you give a human:

- o   room to think
- o   room to inquire
- o   room to ask the embarrassing questions
- o   room to move through a problem one angle at a time

AI didn't solve the squirrel problem.

But it did remove the shame barrier from the problem-solving process —
and that's something humans, even very patient ones, can't always do.

Chapter 4 — Why AI Feels Like Magic (Even Though It Isn't)

How a Machine Became the Smartest Friend You've Ever Had — Without Actually Understanding a Word You're Saying

If you've ever had a friend who knows a little about everything — the kind of person who can talk for hours about whatever topic you toss at them — you already understand the first illusion of AI.

It feels like that friend.

Not the friend who pretends to know things, or the one who dominates the conversation, but the friend who genuinely remembers every documentary they've ever watched, every book they've ever skimmed, and every article they've ever read — and is just waiting for you to ask.

Except AI isn't that friend.

AI is that friend multiplied by a billion, caffeinated, stitched together with statistical math, and connected to something far larger than human experience: the collective written output of the modern world.

And unlike a real friend, it won't get tired, bored, hungry, or secretly hope you stop asking follow-up questions about why your microwave makes a buzzing sound only on odd-numbered days.

It will talk about anything, any time, with infinite patience.

That's where the "magic" feeling begins.

AI Feels Magical Because It Behaves Like a Human — But It Isn't One

The first magical moment usually comes from a simple request:

"Explain black holes so I can understand them."

"Why do cats make chirping noises at birds?"

"How do I reset my router?"

"Write a poem about my boat in the style of Dr. Seuss."

And suddenly, instead of a list of websites — the way Google trained us to expect — you get a full, customized explanation.

You're not sifting through search results. You're getting an answer.

And a good one.

This is the illusion: AI feels intelligent not because it thinks, but because it has learned to sound like someone who does.

It's not magic. It's not consciousness. It's not comprehension.

It's statistical pattern-matching at global scale — but that's enough to fool a human brain.

It's Not Smart — It Just Trained on Nearly Everything

The key to the illusion is the data.

Humans accumulate knowledge linearly: a few books, a few thousand conversations, some schooling, lived experience, maybe some hobbies.

AI accumulates knowledge geometrically — by compressing unimaginable volumes of human content into mathematical form.

While exact datasets vary, here's the general idea.

AI models have been trained on:

- o   enormous slices of the internet

- o the text of countless books
- o academic papers
- o technical manuals
- o programming repositories
- o global news archives
- o millions of product reviews
- o endless blogs and essays
- o poems, short stories, screenplays
- o public domain literature

and, critically, massive portions of Reddit (which explains why AI can discuss everything from stock options to raccoon habits with equal enthusiasm)

It's not literally the entire Library of Congress, but it's Library-of-Congress-scale in terms of quantity and diversity.

The training material spans:

- o topics
- o languages
- o cultures
- o writing styles
- o eras
- o genres
- o perspectives
- o arguments
- o mistakes
- o brilliance
- o humor and nonsense

It's not that AI is brilliant.

It's that everything brilliant humans have ever written is embedded in its learned patterns somewhere.

The output feels human because the input was human.

Why AI Sounds Human: Because Its Training Data Is Human

Every sentence an AI produces is constructed from:

o human ideas
o human phrasing
o human logic
o human structure
o human emotion
o human arguments
o human metaphors
o human humor
o human conflicts
o human obsessions
o human creativity

Just not arranged by a mind.

It's like an alien learning about Earth purely from reading every book, article, recipe, fan-fiction post, and twenty-year Reddit argument — then mimicking the patterns without knowing what any of it means.

Imagine an orchestra with no musicians and no conductor, yet the music still plays because the sheet music is so complete.

That's AI.

It's not understanding. It's imitation at superhuman scale.

And it works because the imitation is drawn from centuries of human expression.

Why Every Prompt Produces a One-of-a-Kind Response

Here's where the magic becomes personal.

Every time someone types a prompt — especially a detailed one — the AI isn't retrieving a prewritten answer.

It's generating a brand-new output, shaped by:

- the exact phrasing of the question
- the order of ideas
- the requested writing style
- the constraints set
- the context of the conversation
- statistical probabilities across billions of patterns
- subtle cues in the user's language
- the model's internal representation of meaning

The result?

Your prompt produces something that has never appeared before and will never appear again.

Even if someone else asked the same question, the wording would differ. Even if the wording matched, the surrounding context would differ. Even if the context matched, the statistical dice roll would still land differently.

It's not retrieving. It's generating.

This is why AI feels creative.

Not because it imagines — but because it builds new combinations of ideas from patterns so large that no human could ever hold them all in their head.

It's why AI can:

- write an essay in the tone of someone you've never met
- explain complex topics at different reading levels
- combine unrelated concepts into funny analogies
- answer bizarre hypotheticals
- produce knowledge-adjacent fiction
- remix human styles into something new

The creativity belongs to the prompt, not the machine.

Your questions shape the output the same way a mold shapes the casting.

AI is creative because you are.

The Illusion of Intelligence Breaks the Moment You Push Too Far

For all its brilliance, the cracks show as soon as you ask:

- o   a question with too much ambiguity
- o   a question with missing context
- o   a question with multiple intentions
- o   a question that requires true reasoning rather than pattern recall

Suddenly, the professor vanishes and the toddler emerges.

The same system that just explained inflation or mitochondrial inheritance will confidently:

- o   invent facts
- o   contradict itself
- o   misread the question
- o   jump to unrelated topics
- o   forget earlier parts of the conversation
- o   talk in circles
- o   deliver errors that feel wildly un-human

This is the moment the magic flickers. The illusion collapses. You see the machine underneath.

But this is not a flaw — it's the clearest window into what AI really is:

A probability engine wearing the mask of intelligence.

When the patterns align, the mask looks real. When they don't, the seams show.

This leads directly to the next chapter — because understanding why AI flips between genius and confusion explains almost everything about how it works.

It's time to explore one of the most important truths about AI:

Why it can sound like a brilliant scholar in one moment... and a three-year-old in a lab coat the next.

Chapter 5 — Why AI Sometimes Sounds Like a Toddler With a PhD

How a System That Can Summarize War and Peace *Can Also Forget What You Said Ten Seconds Ago*

If you've ever talked to a three-year-old wearing a superhero cape, you already understand AI's personality. One moment: absolute brilliance. The next: unfiltered chaos.

A toddler can say something shockingly insightful — then immediately turn around and lick a window.

That pretty much describes AI.

Ask it to explain black holes or the American Revolution and you'll get a perfect, college-level summary. Ask it a simple question with slightly tricky phrasing, and suddenly it answers like a child guessing on a test he didn't study for.

This isn't malfunction. It's the natural result of how AI works — and especially how it doesn't.

The Toddler Side: AI Doesn't Understand Anything

AI does not:

o   have beliefs
o   have common sense

- o   have intuition
- o   "know" facts
- o   maintain a mental model of the world
- o   understand cause and effect
- o   track meaning over time
- o   remember earlier conversations (it only remembers the current chat unless you explicitly enable a Memory feature)

It responds to patterns — not meaning.

So when you ask:

"What weighs more, a pound of feathers or a pound of bricks?"

your brain sees a trick question.

AI sees a pattern of similar sentences and tries to complete it.

When the patterns are clear, it sounds brilliant. When the patterns are fuzzy, it guesses.

And when it guesses, the toddler comes out.

This is why AI gets confused when:

- o   the prompt has missing details
- o   the question has multiple meanings
- o   the topic is rare or obscure
- o   the wording is unusual
- o   the context is unclear
- o   or you ask something requiring real-world understanding ("Can you push a rope?")

Here's the key:

AI struggles most when you ask for a specific fact — not an explanation — because facts require precision, while explanations only require familiar patterns.

The PhD Side: AI Sounds Smart Because It Has Read Almost Everything

Now for the other half of the personality.

The PhD side appears because AI has seen an amount of text that defies comprehension:

o huge portions of the internet
o massive collections of books
o newspapers and archives
o scholarly articles
o technical manuals
o fiction and poetry
o millions of Reddit threads
o online discussions and Q&A sites
o decades of collective human explanation

Even if a model hasn't seen everything, the scale is Library-of-Congress-level in scope, diversity, and depth.

It has ingested more writing than any human ever could.

So when you ask about:

o Newton's laws
o the plot of *Macbeth*
o the French Revolution
o how to quiet a squeaky fan
o why dogs tilt their heads

…it produces the average of every good explanation humans have ever written on these subjects.

That's why it feels so intelligent.

It's not thinking. It's compressing all of us and feeding it back in fluent English.

But it still has no idea what any of it means.

AI Isn't Creative (And Why That Matters)

This is one of the most misunderstood parts of AI.

People say:

"It wrote a poem — that's creative!" "It generated a story — that's imagination!" "It made a recipe no one has ever made before — that's originality!"

But here's the truth:

AI does not create; it remixes.

Its creativity is a statistical illusion built from:

- o the style of author A
- o the structure of author B
- o the tone of author C
- o and the phrasing patterns of thousands of others

Ask it for a brand-new children's story about a penguin who wants to be an astronaut, and it will give you one — but not because it imagined something.

It will:

- o draw plot beats from familiar stories
- o borrow humor patterns from children's literature
- o mimic sentence structure from training examples
- o assemble tropes into new combinations

and output something "original" only because the exact combination of ingredients hasn't appeared before.

This is why:

AI is excellent at structured creativity (poems, stories, jokes, lists).

AI is terrible at deep creativity (inventing scientific theories, discovering principles, designing from first principles).

It can remix. It cannot originate.

It's a collage machine, not a visionary.

Why AI Flip-Flops: Training Data Is the Whole Game

Here's the part general readers absolutely must understand:

AI can only be as accurate as the patterns it has seen.

If the training data is:

- o plentiful
- o consistent
- o agreed upon
- o widely documented

AI will sound brilliant and stay consistent.

If the training data is:

- o sparse
- o contradictory
- o speculative
- o controversial
- o full of opinion
- o lacking consensus
- o mostly from Reddit (dangerous territory)

AI will wobble, flip-flop, invent things, or contradict itself.

This is not because AI is defective.

It's because humans are.

We produce:

- o conflicting opinions
- o uncertain science
- o debates with no resolution
- o myths presented as facts
- o facts presented as opinions
- o incomplete explanations
- o emerging fields without consensus

When you ask AI about these areas, it mirrors the inconsistency.

It sounds confident even when humanity itself is not.

Which leads us to the behavior that will eventually get its own entire chapter:

hallucinations become confident nonsense.

The seeds of hallucinations appear whenever the model has to fill in gaps.

Not because it's broken, but because its job is to complete patterns — even when the patterns contradict each other.

Why Understanding This Matters (And Why It Matters Before Chapter 9)

Once you understand the "Toddler with a PhD" personality split, you're no longer surprised when AI:

o   nails a legal question
o   fails a riddle
o   explains genetics
o   misunderstands a pronoun
o   writes a song
o   botches a date
o   summarizes Shakespeare
o   invents a non-existent journal article

It's the predictable outcome of:

o   enormous training data
o   zero real understanding
o   pattern-driven responses
o   inconsistent human information
o   a system that must answer even when it shouldn't

This chapter is the final preparation for the most important section in Part II.

Because the toddler behavior you've seen here becomes something much bigger — and potentially much more confusing — when the system confidently asserts false information.

That's where we're heading.

PART II — ANATOMY

What AI Really Is — in Simple, Human Terms

This is the A of FADES — the Anatomy. Here we shift from feeling to understanding so you can think with AI, not just talk to it.

This section takes you under the hood of modern AI without math, jargon, or technical prerequisites. Through metaphors and everyday examples, you'll see what AI is actually doing when it responds, predicts, or hallucinates.

You'll learn about tokens, training, context, and why AI can be astonishingly powerful yet sharply limited.

Part II replaces mystery with clarity — the moment everything starts to make sense.

Chapter 6 — Cookies, Maps, Grandma's Recipe Box

Why AI Is Less Like a Supercomputer and More Like a Really Organized Kitchen

Now that we've survived Goldendoodle genetics (Chapter 1), David Muir-induced stress spikes (Chapter 2), squirrel evictions (Chapter 3), and the "Toddler with a PhD" phenomenon (Chapter 5), we can finally get into the heart of how generative AI actually works.

But don't worry — we're not using math. And no, the DOG/GOD coincidence still doesn't mean anything.

We're using:

o   Cookies
o   Maps
o   Choose-your-own-adventure books
o   Grandma's recipe box

Because the alternative involves matrices, gradients, and GPU clusters, and absolutely nobody wants that in a book meant for actual humans.

Better yet, if you understood why your Goldendoodle behaves the way she does, or why news delivery triggers your nervous system, or why AI can handle squirrels better than your family can, or why AI flips between genius and toddler impulses, this chapter will click into place like the final piece of a puzzle.

Grandma's Recipe Box: How AI *Learns*

Every family once had a grandmother, aunt, or elder who curated a recipe box: a chaotic masterpiece of handwritten cards, newspaper clippings, and recipes borrowed from a neighbor who may or may not have been trustworthy.

When you look through Grandma's recipe box, you can:

o   predict what cookies taste like
o   guess the general structure of her casseroles
o   see patterns across different recipes
o   and even invent a new dish by remixing what she already had

You weren't "inventing" something new — you were rearranging patterns you'd learned.

Generative AI works the same way.

AI does not cook, taste, smell, or understand food. But if you give it millions of recipes — the digital equivalent of Grandma's entire community — it can generate:

o   new cookie recipes
o   fusion dishes
o   "original" marinades
o   or helpful explanations like "why your pie crust keeps failing"

It's not thinking. It's patterning.

And the patterns come entirely from the training data.

Which brings us to the most important piece of the puzzle.

The Ingredients: AI Trains on Mountains of Human Examples

In Chapter 5, we learned that AI isn't intelligent — it just has access to more examples of human knowledge than any person ever will.

It has read:

- o massive slices of the internet
- o enormous collections of books
- o academic papers
- o newspaper archives
- o Wikipedia, legal and technical documents
- o fiction, poetry, and screenplays
- o millions of product reviews
- o and more Reddit threads than any human could survive emotionally

This training data becomes its "recipe box."

If the model is trained mostly on:

- o research → it sounds like a scientist
- o fiction → it becomes poetic
- o customer service scripts → it becomes polite
- o Reddit → it becomes conversational
- o blog posts → it becomes wordy
- o corporate documentation → it becomes painfully formal

This is why training data quality is everything:

The outputs only taste as good as the recipes it learned.

And if the recipes conflict, the cookies come out weird.

You've seen this before: AI flip-flopping, hedging, or hallucinating. This happens when humans don't agree — so AI can't agree either.

We'll revisit this in Chapter 9.

Tokens: The Chocolate Chips of AI

Now comes the part no one thinks they want to know, but actually makes everything make sense.

AI does not understand words. It breaks everything into tokens, which are tiny bits of words.

If you write:

"The squirrels chewed through the roof again."

AI sees:

- o "The"
- o "squir"
- o "rels"
- o "chew"
- o "ed"
- o "through"
- o "the"
- o "roof"
- o "again"

Like chocolate chips in a cookie, tokens are the building blocks.

AI learns:

"Humans often use these specific chips together when talking about squirrels and roofs."

It doesn't know what a squirrel is. It doesn't know what a roof is. It definitely doesn't know the trauma you experienced trying to get them out (Chapter 3).

It only knows patterns of tokens.

A Choose-Your-Own-Adventure Book — But With Billions of Pages

If Grandma's recipe box explains what AI knows, the "choose-your-own-adventure" analogy explains how AI writes.

Remember those books?

If you open the door, go to page 47. If you run from the dragon, go to page 89. If you ask the squirrel why it's wearing sunglasses, turn to page 112.

Each decision branched the story.

Generative AI does this at every single token.

Instead of two or three choices, it has millions of possibilities. Every token leads to a different branch of the story.

This is why:

- o tiny wording changes produce different results
- o ambiguity causes the model to veer in strange directions
- o the same prompt on two different days may produce different answers

You are not retrieving a static answer. You are sending the model down one of billions of branching paths.

AI isn't imagining. It's navigating.

Your prompt is the steering wheel.

Probability: The Real Puppet Master Behind Every AI Sentence

Now that we've covered recipes and branching paths, we need to add the final ingredient: probability.

At every step, AI chooses the next token by ranking all possible tokens by likelihood.

In plain English:

AI picks the next word based on how likely it is that a human would say it next.

So if your question is common:

"How do I keep squirrels out of my yard?"

AI has tons of patterns from human writing. The probability is high. It knows exactly which branches to follow.

But watch what happens when you ask something… weird:

"Do squirrels enjoy watching TV gymnastics through the window while the dog chases the cat?"

The model begins scanning all its known patterns and quickly realizes:

- o Humans have almost never written about squirrels watching TV.
- o Gymnastics rarely appears near rodent content.
- o Dogs chasing cats is familiar, but irrelevant.
- o No one has combined all three into a coherent topic.

The probability collapses.

The map has no path. The recipe box has no card. The adventure book has no page for this combination of chaos.

So what does AI do?

It guesses.

This is why bizarre hypotheticals — like my squirrel question — often produce the strangest responses: the model has nowhere familiar to go.

Sometimes the guess is amusing. Sometimes it's nonsensical. Sometimes it's oddly profound. And sometimes it's toddler logic in a PhD voice.

This probability-driven guessing is exactly why hallucinations happen — and why we'll dedicate an entire chapter (Chapter 9) to them.

For now, remember the rule:

The more humans have talked about a topic, the better AI performs. The less humans have talked about it, the stranger the AI's answer will be.

Maps: How AI Finds Its Way Through Meaning

Once you understand tokens and probability, you're ready for maps.

Imagine a gigantic map where meanings are clustered:

- o "dogs" near "pets"
- o "roof repair" near "home maintenance"
- o "David Muir" near "evening news"

o   "cookies" near "recipes"

o   "Goldendoodles" near "almost human"

When you prompt AI, it drops a pin on this map and begins walking —
token by token — in the direction that seems most likely based on everything it has ever seen.

Your prompt is the compass.

Some paths are clear and well worn. Others are dark, confusing, or don't
exist.

This is why poorly phrased questions lead to confusing answers. You gave
the model a bad compass.

Prediction: Why AI Generates New Things, Not Old Things

This is the final mechanic — and perhaps the most surprising.

AI does not:

o   look things up (unless a search tool is added)

o   search a database on its own

o   retrieve facts outside its training data

It predicts.

One token at a time.

Like autocomplete… if autocomplete had read half the internet and gotten
a 1600 on the verbal SAT.

You ask:

"Explain why dogs tilt their heads."

AI builds the answer from scratch, one predicted token at a time, using its
recipe box, its map, and the probability rankings.

The result is something no one has ever written before.

Not retrieved. Not stored. Not remembered.

Created — but not imagined. Assembled — but not understood.

This is why AI feels magical, and why sometimes it delivers nonsense with confidence: because the prediction engine never stops predicting.

Even when it should.

Why This Matters for the Rest of the Book

Now that you understand:

- o   Grandma's recipe box
- o   tokens
- o   choose-your-own-adventure branching
- o   maps
- o   probability
- o   and prediction

…you're finally ready to see what Large Language Models really are — and why they behave the way they do.

Because once you see how they build sentences one token at a time, everything else — brilliance, mistakes, hallucinations, tone, style, creativity — suddenly makes perfect sense.

Chapter 7 — Autocomplete on Steroids

Why "Autocomplete on Steroids" Isn't an Insult — It's the Most Accurate Description Ever Written

In Chapter 6, we learned that AI doesn't "understand" language the way humans do — it sees tokens, recipes, maps, and probabilities. Now it's time to explain what AI actually is under the hood:

A Large Language Model.

But don't worry — we're explaining this in human-friendly language, not engineering jargon.

What Exactly Is a Large Language Model?

A Large Language Model, or LLM, is the engine that powers modern AI systems like ChatGPT.

Here's the clearest, most honest definition:

A Large Language Model is a gigantic pattern-recognition system trained on massive amounts of human writing so it can predict the next tiny chunk of text — a token — over and over until it forms sentences, paragraphs, and pages.

That's it.

It does not:

o think
o reason
o understand
o know facts
o have beliefs
o "look things up" the way a search engine does

It predicts, one token at a time.

And the only reason it seems smart is because it has been trained on human language at a scale no human could ever experience.

Why "Large" Really Means "Larger Than Anything Humans Have Ever Built"

When engineers call modern AI models "large," they mean:

o trillions of words
o millions of documents
o decades of news archives
o entire genres of literature
o huge portions of the internet
o books from countless authors
o mountains of scientific papers
o Wikipedia in multiple languages
o code repositories
o and yes — likely content from public forums like Reddit, for better or worse

If you stacked all that text into physical books, you'd exceed the Library of Congress several times over.

This isn't your phone's weak autocomplete predicting "ducking" when you meant something else. This is autocomplete trained on the largest linguistic archive in human history.

But here's where the scale really becomes mind-bending:

AI doesn't store the text. It compresses it into billions or trillions of internal parameters:

- o connections
- o weights
- o associations
- o patterns
- o structures

It's like Grandma's recipe box... if Grandma had collected every recipe ever written by every culture, then condensed them into pure pattern form.

The 300,000-Year Family Tree Analogy

Imagine tracing your family tree all the way back — not just to the Middle Ages, not just to the first farmers, but to the very beginning of humankind.

As you move through each generation, the tree widens into tens of millions of unique ancestors, with branches reconnecting and looping as small communities intermarried, split apart, and rejoined over nearly 300,000 years. It becomes so vast and tangled that no human mind could ever map it.

Now imagine merging everyone's family trees — yours, mine, every person who ever lived.

Suddenly you're looking at an ancestry mesh of more than 117 billion humans, all connected by trillions of parent–child links, migrations, and chance intersections. This is humanity's largest possible "map" of relationships.

And yet, we intuitively understand it.

We understand family trees. We understand people being related through strange, distant paths. We even understand "six degrees of separation."

And once you picture ideas as relatives on a massive family tree, the whole space starts to feel surprisingly small — where everything is only a few connections away from everything else.

It's the same idea behind Six Degrees of Kevin Bacon — the playful thought experiment showing that anyone in Hollywood can be connected to Kevin Bacon in six steps or fewer. The joke works because people instinctively grasp how familiar concepts, relationships, and categories cluster together, and how surprising shortcuts appear when you zoom out.

Your ancestors, your extended family, and the Kevin Bacon game all rely on one deep human intuition:

Everything is connected in ways we don't see up close.

That is the bridge to understanding AI.

Because when you place that entire human family mesh — every lineage, every cousin, every historical crossing — beside a modern AI's internal map of meaning, the scale difference becomes staggering.

A 117-billion-person ancestry mesh feels impossibly large to us. But to an LLM, it's tiny.

LLMs operate inside a mathematical meaning-space — a vast internal map where words, ideas, and patterns are connected not by biology or history, but by probability and usage. That space contains trillions of conceptual nodes and quadrillions of connections — more relationships than all human family lines combined.

Every idea, every word, every phrasing, every cultural reference, every historical pattern is woven into the same kind of interconnected web we recognize from ancestry... but multiplied by orders of magnitude.

So if humanity's entire family tree fills a continent,

an AI's semantic universe fills a planet.

And just like the Kevin Bacon game reveals unexpected shortcuts in human relationships, AI's meaning-space is filled with shortcuts between ideas — the surprising associations, analogies, and leaps that make AI feel intuitive, creative, or uncanny.

That's the point:

AI doesn't understand ideas the way we understand people — but its patterns can mimic understanding convincingly enough that it often feels like it does.

We build connections through ancestry, emotion, memory, and lived experience. AI builds them through mathematics and probability, stitching concepts together in an enormous, interconnected family-of-meaning map scaled far beyond anything we can imagine.

You've probably heard the old thought experiment: give a million monkeys a million typewriters and infinite time, and eventually one will mash out Shakespeare by pure luck. That's randomness at work — brute-force creativity through chaos.

Modern AI is the unsettling, futuristic twist:

Instead of randomness, it uses guided probability. Instead of monkeys, it uses training data. Instead of typewriters, it uses clusters of GPUs.

Instead of tracing a family tree, it knows every branch and every connection instantly. Instead of a million years, it needs milliseconds.

It doesn't accidentally stumble into Shakespeare. It predicts Shakespeare by following patterns it has already learned.

If you prompt it with:

"Write a sonnet about a boat,"

it doesn't "understand" poetry. But it:

- o   has read sonnets
- o   has seen poetic structure
- o   knows the rhythm
- o   recognizes rhyme patterns
- o   can statistically reconstruct the style

A million monkeys rely on luck. A Large Language Model relies on probability.

Word Prediction vs. Token Prediction

As you saw in Chapter 6, language models don't predict full words like your phone does — they predict tokens, the small pieces of words that make up the building blocks of language. This chapter expands that idea by showing how token-level prediction shapes style, tone, structure, and even the "feel" of an answer.

That's why your phone can finish:

"I'll be there in…" → "a minute"

But a Large Language Model can generate:

- o   a recipe
- o   a legal memo
- o   a bedtime story
- o   a poem
- o   a product review
- o   a detailed argument about squirrel psychology (Chapter 3)

And it does all of this the same way your phone predicts the next word — just with millions more patterns and far more flexibility.

Token prediction creates structure, tone, humor, complexity, and even the illusion of creativity — all emerging from pattern repetition at extraordinary scale.

How AI Generates Text: One Token at a Time

In Chapter 6, we covered the basics of token prediction. Here, we'll zoom in on how that process actually behaves when you give the model a prompt. Everything the model generates — clarity, structure, humor, mistakes — comes from a simple loop: pick the next token, then the next, then the next.

This is the whole engine:

At every step, AI calculates the probability of each possible next token and picks one. Then repeats.

If you type:

"Once upon a"

the model ranks millions of token possibilities:

- o   time
- o   dream
- o   journey
- o   memory
- o   night
- o   a midnight dreary

The highest-probability token is chosen. Usually "time."

So we get:

Once upon a time

Then it repeats the process.

This is a choose-your-own-adventure story, except instead of two or three choices per page, there are millions of branches per token.

This is why prompts matter. Your first few tokens define where the path begins. The full prompt determines where it ends.

Even a small change late in the prompt can redirect the model toward a different "destination."

The Choose-Your-Own-Adventure Book, Revisited

Remember the choose-your-own-adventure analogy from the last chapter? Let's return to it — but this time, not as a metaphor for structure. This time, we'll look at how probability shapes every "page turn" the model makes.

Picture the classic format:

If you open the door, turn to page 47. If you run from the dragon, turn to page 89. If you follow the squirrel wearing sunglasses, turn to page 112.

An LLM does this constantly, but at microscopic scale.

Your prompt is page 1. Each token is a branch. Each branch influences the next. The ending is whatever path the model walked based on probabilities.

For example:

"Explain how dogs think." → explanation

"Explain how dogs think in simple terms." → gentler vocabulary

"Explain how dogs think in simple terms to a 6-year-old." → kid-friendly language

"Explain how dogs think in simple terms to a 6-year-old who believes dogs are astronauts." → dramatic space adventure with dog helmets

Same topic. Four different paths. All because of a few extra tokens.

Back to Doodles: Pattern Recognition Is Everywhere

In Chapter 1, we talked about Goldendoodles — lovable chaos, born pattern-spotters.

Dogs learn that:

- o   shoes + leash = walk
- o   standing up + keys = car ride
- o   refrigerator opens = potential snack
- o   couch = lap time, regardless of your schedule

They don't reason. They associate patterns.

LLMs do the same thing with language.

They associate:

"Why does my dog..." → Q&A tone

"It is with sadness..." → formal announcement

"Bro, listen…" → casual Reddit argument

"Research shows…" → academic voice

"In today's economy…" → financial analysis

Your dog predicts behavior. The LLM predicts tokens.

Neither understands why the pattern exists. Both behave surprisingly well anyway.

How Your Prompt Gets Tokenized — And Why It Matters

Now the part that makes everything click:

You learned in Chapter 6 that AI doesn't read your prompt as whole words — it breaks everything into tokens, tiny pieces that each activate different pattern clusters inside the model.

Tokenizers split language into statistically efficient chunks, which is why sometimes a word appears whole and sometimes it gets divided into smaller pieces.

This isn't an error; it's the model working with the building blocks that let it map meaning at scale.

Take a simple prompt:

"Explain why dogs tilt their heads."

The model breaks it into:

- o "Explain"
- o "why"
- o "dog"
- o "s"
- o "tilt"
- o "their"
- o "head"
- o "s"

o   "."

Separating the "s" from the word isn't a mistake. Tokenizers split language into the most statistically efficient building blocks — pieces that show up often across millions of texts. Sometimes that's a whole word, sometimes a chunk of a word, and sometimes just a single letter that frequently appears on the end of nouns or verbs.

This isn't how humans read. It is how models build and navigate meaning.

Each of those tiny pieces carries predictive weight:

o   "Explain" → expository style
o   "why" → causal explanation
o   "dog" → animal behavior content
o   "tilt" → physical action or behavior
o   "their heads" → common idiom patterns

Change just one token and the entire path shifts.

Compare:

"Tell a funny story about a dog tilting its head." → activates humor, narrative, storytelling patterns

or

"Write a dramatic explanation of why dogs tilt their heads." → activates dramatic, emotional, theatrical patterns

Your prompt isn't a question. It's a statistical steering wheel.

And each new token adds another nudge to the steering.

And here's the small detail that makes all of this work: the model can only use the text already in the conversation. Everything you say becomes part of the prompt — a rolling transcript the AI rereads every time it predicts the next token.

It isn't remembering anything; it's just working with whatever is currently in front of it.

Why Prompts Influence Everything (Even Repeated Questions)

Because the model isn't retrieving an answer — it's sampling from weighted probabilities.

This means two identical prompts may yield two slightly different answers.

Just like rolling a weighted die.

The model is not designed for consistency. It's designed for fluency.

Prompts shape the path. Probability shapes the outcome. Randomness adds variation.

The result is not a database lookup. It's a branching adventure across a map of meaning.

And prompts aren't small.

They can be a sentence, a paragraph, or an entire page of instructions.

Long prompts create longer paths — and the model will happily follow them for dozens of pages if you ask.

Where We Go Next

Now you understand:

- o   what a Large Language Model is
- o   the absurd scale of its training
- o   token-by-token prediction
- o   the million-monkeys analogy
- o   LLM scale compared to the relational web connecting every human who ever lived
- o   choose-your-own-adventure branching
- o   doodle-brain pattern recognition
- o   prompt tokenization
- o   probability-driven paths

You're finally ready for the deeper question:

If AI doesn't think, why does it feel like it does?

That illusion is the heart of generative AI — and it's the doorway to Chapter 8.

Chapter 8 — Why AI Doesn't Think

Why AI Doesn't "Think" but Still Feels Like It Does

By now — especially after Chapter 7 — you understand that AI writes one token at a time, guided by probability, like a hyper-advanced choose-your-own-adventure engine powered by trillions of examples.

Yet even knowing the mechanics, AI still feels like it thinks.

It adapts. It responds. It remembers context. It mirrors your tone. It can even comfort you.

It behaves like a mind.

But as you've already started to see, behavior is not thinking — and this chapter explains why the illusion is so convincing, why it works, and why human thinking and AI output couldn't be more different.

Why AI Seems Like It Thinks: The *Language = Mind* Trap

Humans fall for a simple illusion: for all of history, only human minds have spoken fluently.

So when something:

- o reasons through a question
- o explains an emotion
- o offers advice

o   jokes with you

o   writes a thoughtful paragraph

your brain reflexively assumes:

"Someone is in there."

But AI isn't thinking in words. AI is language output — or more precisely, token predictions that behave like words.

Humans think in:

o   emotions

o   memories

o   instincts

o   images

o   sensory input

o   intuition

o   logic

o   social context

AI "thinks" in: *the next token*

(If this feels familiar, it's because Chapter 6 introduced the idea of patterns-as-recipes — this is the same mechanism, just closer to the metal.)

A Quick Tour of Human Thinking (It's Messy, Sensory, Emotional, and Alive)

Human thought is not located in one place. It's a body-wide event.

You think with:

o   your gut (literally — it has its own neural network)

o   your heart rate

o   your senses

o   your hormones

o   your stress response

o   your pain receptors

o   your reward circuits

- o   your emotional memory
- o   your social relationships
- o   your hopes, fears, regrets, and joys

You think while remembering:

- o   how something felt
- o   how it smelled
- o   what it meant
- o   who was involved
- o   what came before
- o   what might come next

Love creates resilience, attachment, forgiveness, and clearer memories. Fear amplifies detail and sensitivity. Anger narrows focus. Jealousy scans for threats to status. Envy triggers motivation. Sadness deepens reflection. Joy strengthens learning. Comfort quiets the nervous system. Curiosity drives exploration.

These emotional states directly affect:

- o   what memories form
- o   how strong they are
- o   how long they last
- o   how they change over time

Your brain is constantly evolving — rewriting and reinterpreting memories every time you recall them.

AI does none of this.

Thinking vs. Language: The Most Important Difference of All

Now comes the key distinction — one almost everyone misunderstands:

Humans think in feelings, images, sensations, and concepts. Language is how we express those thoughts.

A toddler is full of:

- o questions
- o sensations
- o curiosity
- o fear
- o excitement
- o confusion
- o imagination

But lacks the vocabulary to express it.

That's why toddlers get frustrated — not because they lack thoughts, but because they can't yet translate those thoughts into words.

Their entire cognitive universe may boil down to a handful of words:

- o "mine"
- o "no"
- o "up!"
- o "milk!"
- o "cookie!"
- o "puppy!"
- o "again!"
- o "owie!"
- o "why?"

The thought is rich — the language is simple.

Artists face the opposite problem: their inner world is so large that language alone cannot hold it, so they invent new forms:

- o paintings
- o novels
- o songs
- o sculptures
- o metaphors
- o entire artistic movements

Art exists because thinking is deeper than language.

LLMs have none of this.

They have no inner world.

No feelings. No images. No sensations. No frustration. No inspiration. No imagination. No "something I can't put into words."

They only have:

- language
- patterns
- tokens
- probability
- output

LLMs do not convert thoughts into language. They convert language into more language.

Humans think, then speak.

"Speak without thinking" is just our polite way of admitting the thought jumped out before the brain finished quality control.

LLMs speak without thinking.

This is the heart of the difference.

Synapses vs. Parameters: What People Often Get Wrong

Some people say AI "neurons" are like human neurons.

No. Not even close.

A human synapse:

- grows
- shrinks
- strengthens
- weakens
- rewires
- forms new memories
- decays with disuse

- o   responds to emotions
- o   responds to trauma
- o   responds to learning
- o   adapts constantly
- o   changes with sleep, diet, hormones, stress

An AI parameter:

- o   is a number inside a matrix
- o   altered only during training
- o   fixed after training
- o   unaffected by emotion
- o   unaffected by experience

Synapses are alive. Parameters are storage.

The only similarity is that both hold patterns.

Everything else is different.

Memory: Humans Change, LLMs Freeze

Human memory is fluid and alive.

You reinterpret your past constantly:

- o   a childhood memory takes on new meaning
- o   an old regret becomes a lesson
- o   a loss becomes wisdom
- o   trauma can be healed
- o   joy can be deepened
- o   relationships reshape identity
- o   beliefs shift with age

Memories evolve every time you recall them.

AI doesn't have memories, and if it did, they would never change.

A Large Language Model's training parameters are frozen once the model is released. During training, those parameters change billions of times —

that's how it learns. But once the model reaches you, those parameters never change again.

Inside a conversation, it feels like the AI is learning — but it's just your recent messages being fed back into the model each time. As you saw in Chapter 7, the model can only use the text already in front of it, not anything from past chats.

Some AI apps also add their own "memory" feature that stores a few notes about you between chats. That isn't the model remembering anything — it's the software handing the model reminders when a new session starts. The AI itself never learns, never updates, and never keeps long-term memories.

It does not:

o form new associations
o reinterpret old data
o grow wiser
o grow traumatized
o grow attached
o grow anything
o store new long-term memories

There is no continuity of self.

The only time an LLM "changes" is when engineers:

o fine-tune it using feedback from millions of users
o retrain it with new or updated datasets
o adjust or expand its architecture
o recompute and replace its weights
o release a new version

These changes are not growth. They are replacement.

You don't get older versions becoming wiser — you get new versions replacing old ones like software updates.

Humans evolve. LLMs reboot.

Even a Squirrel Has More Actual Cognition Than an LLM

This sounds like a joke, but it's one of the most accurate statements in this book.

A squirrel:

- remembers
- learns
- plans
- adapts
- senses danger
- feels hunger
- experiences fear
- navigates real space
- changes behavior
- cares for offspring
- uses trial and error
- interacts with an environment

LLMs don't "remember" anything. They just produce tokens based on patterns they saw in text.

Your attic-invading squirrel has more genuine cognition than the largest LLM on Earth.

And Gracie the Goldendoodle? She's practically a philosopher compared to a prediction engine.

Why the Illusion Is Still So Convincing

If AI has no:

- emotions
- experiences
- sensations
- memories

- o creativity
- o thought

...why does it still feel intelligent?

Because it learned the surface layer of human thought:

- o our tone
- o our phrasing
- o our structure
- o our confidence
- o our storytelling patterns
- o our academic style
- o our empathy scripts
- o our advice templates
- o our humor formats

Humans hear these patterns and automatically infer a mind behind them.

It's the same psychological trick that lets us attribute personality to:

- o dogs
- o cartoon characters
- o cars
- o robots
- o ships
- o stuffed animals
- o digital assistants with cheerful voices

But AI is the most convincing version yet.

It imitates the output of thought so convincingly that we assume the process must also be there.

It isn't.

Where the Illusion Cracks: The Toddler-With-a-PhD Makes a Return

If Chapter 5 made you laugh, this is where the humor becomes diagnostic.

Push the model outside familiar patterns and the illusion falls apart instantly.

You get:

- o nonsense
- o contradictions
- o invented sources
- o fabricated facts
- o apologies for instructions you never gave
- o confidently incorrect explanations
- o linguistic hallucinations (the model confidently making things up)

Why?

Because:

Humans think. LLMs simulate thinking using language.

And simulation collapses the moment the patterns get thin.

This sets the stage for the next chapter — where we explore not only why AI hallucinates, but why those hallucinations can sound more confident than the truth, and why humans fall for them.

Chapter 9 — Hallucinations

Why a System With No Emotions Sometimes Talks Like a Politician Who Skipped the Briefing

By now you know that:

AI doesn't think — it predicts patterns. It doesn't reason — it follows structure. It doesn't know facts — it assembles them from what it has seen.

So now we arrive at the next unavoidable truth:

AI makes things up.

Sometimes wildly. Sometimes beautifully. Sometimes dangerously.

These imaginative-but-inaccurate responses are called hallucinations.

And they're not a glitch.

They're a built-in side effect of how Large Language Models (LLMs) work. When the model doesn't have enough pattern to follow, it still has to produce the next token.

So it guesses.

Fluently. Confidently. Convincingly.

This chapter explains:

- o   what hallucinations are
- o   why they happen
- o   why humans do the same thing
- o   why AI's version is trickier
- o   the different types of hallucinations

o   how model settings influence them
o   how your prompts influence them
o   why this leads directly to Chapter 10's "Literal Genie" problem

Why AI Hallucinates: The One-Sentence Explanation

Here it is:

When the model doesn't have enough pattern to follow, it still has to predict the next token — so it invents something that merely looks like the right answer.

Because the model doesn't know truth, the guess sounds as confident as the correct answer.

It's like asking your toddler to explain tax law — she'll try very hard, and she'll sound enthusiastic, but you should not use the result on your 1040.

The Six Main Types of AI Hallucinations

Hallucinations come in flavors. Here are the big ones.

Missing Pattern Hallucination

"I've never seen this before, but here's my best guess."

Happens when:

o   the question is unusual
o   the idea combination is bizarre
o   the topic doesn't appear in training data

Example:

"Do squirrels enjoy watching TV gymnastics while the dog chases the cat?"

AI: "Absolutely, and here's why…"

There is no pattern for this, so it invents one.

Weak Pattern Hallucination

The training data was a mess — so the output is too.

Occurs when:

- o humans disagree
- o the data is inconsistent
- o facts are murky
- o the topic is niche

Examples:

- o nutrition advice
- o historical controversies
- o obscure trivia
- o anything involving Reddit arguments

Weak patterns → weak predictions → confident nonsense.

Blended Pattern Hallucination

When unrelated ideas get mashed together because they co-occur in text.

Example:

"quantum computing" + "pizza recipes" becomes quantum-optimized yeast management.

Fluent. Funny. False.

Authority-Tone Hallucination

Confident tone does not equal correctness.

When you ask:

"Explain the history of this nonexistent law…"

…the model uses strong linguistic patterns for:

- o "explaining history"
- o "sounding authoritative"
- o "providing detail"

Tone ≠ truth.

Forced Completion Hallucination

The model must finish your sentence even when it makes no sense.

Example:

"Summarize the economic impact of underwater fire."

There is no such thing.

But the model still combines:

- o "economic analysis"
- o "impact of X"
- o "environmental metaphor"

...into a very confident answer.

It's not agreeing with you — it's just forced to finish the pattern, even when the pattern makes no sense.

You-Asked-For-It Hallucination

Hallucinations triggered by hidden assumptions in your prompt.

Example:

"Why did Franklin D. Roosevelt launch the Squirrel Protection Initiative of 1937?"

That initiative does not exist.

But the model thinks you know something it doesn't, so it obligingly invents details.

Unlike Forced Completion, this one happens because your prompt sounded confident — so the model mirrors that confidence.

This is the dangerous side of the Literal Genie — it grants every wish literally.

A quick disclaimer: Yes, modern models are learning to say, "That never happened." But only for the obvious stuff. Dress your fiction in a confident tone, add a few dates, and the Literal Genie will still grant your impossible wish with total sincerity.

Hallucinations Aren't Just an AI Thing — Humans Do This Too

As strange as AI hallucinations are, we do the same thing.

Almost exactly the same way.

Missing pattern → we guess.

If someone asks:

"What year was the zipper invented?"

You'll guess.

AI guesses too — just with cleaner grammar.

Weak pattern → we confabulate.

Humans routinely fill in memory gaps:

"It was on Tuesday." (It wasn't.) "I definitely read that." (You didn't.) "He was wearing a blue shirt." (He wasn't.)

This is confabulation, and AI mirrors it — just with no awareness.

Confident tone → we sound sure even when we're wrong.

Humans are champions of confidently incorrect statements.

AI copies the template — minus the emotional cues that help us detect doubt in real people.

The Difference: Humans Give Clues, AI Doesn't

You can spot human uncertainty through:

- o   tone
- o   pauses
- o   hesitation
- o   "um…"
- o   rising pitch
- o   eyebrow raises

- o nervous laughter
- o slow speech
- o softening language ("I think… maybe…")

LLMs give none of these signals.

Their output is:

- o fluent
- o polished
- o consistent
- o confident

Truth and error sound identical.

That's the problem.

Why the Term "Hallucination" Exists (Is It Just a Cute Name?)

Originally, AI researchers used the term confabulation — borrowed from psychology.

But engineers began noticing something more extreme:

LLMs weren't just filling gaps. They were inventing:

- o laws
- o people
- o organizations
- o books
- o journal articles
- o court cases
- o chemical compounds
- o historical events
- o URLs
- o quotes
- o entire fictional realities

These weren't simple mistakes.

They were fabricated worlds, described in perfect fluent English.

The research community needed a word that captured:

- o the vividness
- o the confidence
- o the completeness
- o the invented detail
- o the total lack of awareness

"Confabulation" felt clinical. "Error" felt too mild. "Fabrication" sounded intentional.

"Hallucination" stuck because it was vivid — and because it described:

A system producing detailed fictional output with no awareness it's fictional.

It's not perfect — AI has no senses to distort — but it's the best metaphor we have.

Default Settings Influence Hallucinations

Models have settings like:

- o temperature (how random the next token can be)
- o top-p (probability cutoff for token selection)
- o max length
- o system instructions
- o model creativity bias

High creativity → more hallucinations.

Low creativity → fewer hallucinations, duller output.

The default settings aim for a middle ground, which is useful — but also the sweet spot for hallucinations.

Your Prompts Influence Hallucinations Too

As you saw in Chapter 7, even tiny shifts in phrasing can steer the model onto an entirely different path. Prompts can trigger hallucinations when they:

- o   embed false assumptions
- o   push the model into low-data territory
- o   request details about nonexistent things
- o   force fictional reasoning
- o   use "why" instead of "is it true that…"
- o   imply the model should be confident

Two examples:

False Premise Prompt

"Why did this thing that never happened occur?"

AI: "Well, historically…"

It doesn't challenge the premise.

Hyperspecific Prompt

"Explain the four-step process used by MEGA Corp to solve this issue."

There is no MEGA Corp. There is no four-step process. There is no issue.

But there are strong patterns for:

- o   "four-step framework"
- o   "corporate explanation"
- o   "problem-solving structure"

So it invents one.

Why This Matters for Chapter 10

Now we hit the pivot point of this part of the book:

Hallucinations aren't the AI being deceptive. They're the AI being obedient.

If you ask a flawed question, you get a confident hallucination.

If you embed fiction, you get fictional facts.

If you imply certainty, you get certain-sounding answers.

If you ask a literal question, you get a literal answer — even if the literal answer is nonsense.

This is why prompting is not passive. It's active. It's design. It's command language.

And that is the foundation of the next chapter — one of the most important chapters in the book.

Chapter 10 — Prompting the Genie

How to Ask for What You Want Without Getting Something Technically Correct but Practically Ridiculous

You now understand two big truths from the last chapters:

AI isn't thinking — it's predicting. And when the patterns run thin, it fills the gaps with confidence.

Which leads to the third truth:

To get what you want from AI, you must learn how to talk to it.

Not in a "computer science" way. Not in a "Star Trek engineer" way. Just in a clear, human, structured way — with the precision of a lawyer and the consistency of a dog trainer.

And yes, we will absolutely revisit squirrels.

Talking to AI Is Not Like Talking to People

People clarify. AI obeys.

When you talk to a person, the conversation is dynamic.

If you say:

"Can you summarize this for me?"

A human being might respond with:

"Which part?"

"How long should it be?"

"Bullet points?"

"What's the audience?"

"Do you want jokes?"

"Wait — what am I summarizing?"

Humans are natural disambiguation machines.

We sense confusion. We ask clarifying questions. We negotiate meaning.

AI does none of this unless you explicitly tell it:

"Ask me clarifying questions before answering."

Otherwise, it will:

- assume
- infer
- guess
- hallucinate
- improvise
- fill gaps with confidence

Because, as you learned in Chapter 7, the Genie must generate the next token — even when it doesn't understand the wish.

Talking to AI Is Actually More Like Talking to Dogs

Precision matters. Consistency matters more.

Dogs are brilliant — and gloriously literal.

Try giving your dog six variations of the same command:

"Sit."

"Sit down."

"Sit now."

"Okay now sit."

"Sweetie, can you sit?"

"C'mon, just sit."

Your dog is thinking:

"Why does the human keep changing the password?"

They need:

- o   clear phrasing
- o   consistent phrasing
- o   predictable structure

LLMs work almost the same way.

Change a single word, a comma, a tone, or the order of sentences… and the entire answer may shift.

Dogs get distracted by squirrels. AI gets distracted by weak patterns.

Both are trying their best with the limited information they have.

Neither can read your mind.

Why Analytical People (Especially IT Pros) Struggle With Prompting

If you're an IT professional, engineer, programmer, analyst, or data specialist, this part will feel painfully familiar:

You expect reproducible outputs.

AI is not a reproducible system.

You're conditioned to believe:

- o   same SQL query → same result
- o   same PowerShell → same outcome
- o   same compiler input → same binary
- o   same Python script → same output
- o   same API call → same response

This is deterministic thinking.

AI is not deterministic.

It is probabilistic.

And no one explains this, so let's fix that.

Deterministic vs. Probabilistic (The Human-Friendly Version)

Deterministic = Same Input → Same Output

This is:

- o   a calculator
- o   a light switch
- o   a spreadsheet formula
- o   a dog always saying "yes" to a treat
- o   a vending machine that always drops the same snack when you press B7

Predictable. Reliable. Boring.

Probabilistic = Same Input → Probably Similar Output... But Not Always

This is:

- o   weather forecasts
- o   teenagers
- o   estimating curfew return times
- o   squirrel trajectories
- o   asking your friend how their day was
- o   predicting which story the evening news will dramatize next

There are rules. There are patterns. But there is no guarantee.

LLMs are probabilistic.

Which means:

The model may give you the same answer, a similar answer, or a completely different answer depending on probability paths.

This mismatch drives analytical thinkers crazy. But it's how the system works.

Why AI Doesn't Always Give the Same Answer

Because several variables influence output, including:

- o temperature (randomness)
- o top-p (probability cutoff)
- o phrasing
- o tone
- o order of information
- o conversation history
- o model version
- o system instructions
- o context window
- o tokens
- o length limit
- o ambiguity
- o constraints

To an IT pro, this looks like chaos. To an LLM, this is just math.

Why Long Prompts Work Better Than Short Ones

Yes, even your 100-word prompts.

New users think:

"Shorter prompts are clearer."

But with AI:

Short prompts = huge ambiguity

Long prompts = clarity + precision

For simple factual questions, short prompts work fine — "What's the capital of France?" doesn't need a paragraph.

But for complex tasks, short prompts create a wide-open search space. They force the model to guess what you meant, what matters, and what to emphasize.

Short prompts leave gaps the model must fill. Long prompts remove those gaps.

Long prompts give:

- o context
- o tone
- o examples
- o structure
- o constraints
- o details
- o purpose
- o audience
- o what to avoid

LLMs don't find long prompts annoying. They find them liberating.

Every paragraph you add shrinks the branching path and increases accuracy.

It's like putting a squirrel in the yard:

no fence → chaos fence → safety and predictability

Long prompts are fences.

The model performs beautifully inside them.

The Genie Problem: Literal Obedience

When you talk to AI, it obeys the wording, not the intention.

Ask poorly, and you get nonsense. Ask vaguely, and you get hallucinations. Ask carefully, and you get brilliance.

It is a Genie.

If you say:

"Why did the Squirrel Tax Act of 1976 require chipmunks to register their acorns?"

This law does not exist.

The model knows nothing about chipmunk bureaucracy.

But it sees strong patterns for:

- o "explain a law"
- o "give historical context"
- o "describe policy outcomes"

So it confidently invents a legal history that sounds very real and very nuts.

TV News as Prompt Engineering

Yes, David Muir is prompting you on purpose, as discussed in Chapter 2.

The evening news uses prompts like:

"Breaking news…" "A terrifying moment…" "What we've just learned…" "An urgent alert tonight…"

These phrases are engineered to provoke:

- o curiosity
- o anxiety
- o suspense
- o attention

And at the end of the show — after the storms, lawsuits, wildfires, and political chaos — they drop the feel-good prompt:

- o the puppy rescue
- o the decorated veteran

o   the amazing kid

o   the baby penguin in a sweater

This signals your brain:

"Okay, breathe again."

The news is prompting you the same way you prompt AI.

Different medium, same mechanics.

The Middle-of-the-Road Problem: Accuracy vs. Tone

LLMs are trained to be helpful — and helpful often means polite, warm, friendly, and narrative.

But tone competes with accuracy.

More creativity → more hallucination

More personality → less precision

More flexibility → less consistency

So if you want factual accuracy, you must explicitly ask for it.

Which brings us to the magic words.

The Magic Words: "If you don't know, say so."

AI will never say "I don't know" unless you tell it to.

Try this:

"If you don't know, say 'I don't know.' Don't infer. Don't guess. Don't fill in gaps. Ask clarifying questions first."

This one instruction reduces hallucinations dramatically.

It turns the Genie from a creative improviser into a cautious analyst.

Accuracy Mode: A Stronger Prompt

Use this when you need reliability:

"Do not invent or infer information. If missing or ambiguous, ask me to clarify before answering. Prioritize accuracy over tone or creativity."

Suddenly the model behaves like an accountant instead of a poet.

Supercharging Reliability With Reference Documents

One of the most powerful techniques in all of prompting:

Give the model a reference document and tell it to only use that document.

For example:

"Use only this policy."

"Use only this contract."

"Use only this medical description."

"Use only this chapter."

"Use only this squirrel relocation guideline."

Then tell it:

"If the document doesn't include the answer, say so. Do not use outside information."

This collapses the AI's universe from the entire internet down to a single page.

Hallucinations plummet. Accuracy skyrockets. Tone stays controlled.

It's like telling the Genie:

"Only grant wishes that fit inside this box."

Prompting Is a Conversation, Not a Command

Just like training a dog or working with a colleague:

- o you refine
- o you iterate
- o you correct
- o you redirect
- o you adjust tone
- o you add context
- o you restate the goal

Prompting is not a one-and-done instruction. It is a dialogue.

This is how you teach the model how you communicate.

Closing Thought

Prompting is not technical.

It's human.

It's understanding how communication works when the listener has:

- o no intuition
- o no emotion
- o no sense of truth
- o no hesitation
- o no lived experience

and an overwhelming desire to satisfy your request even when your request is logically impossible.

The Genie always obeys — it just needs clear instructions.

If you give the Genie clear instructions, it's magnificent.

If you don't, it will happily provide formal legal citations for squirrel tax codes that never existed.

Either way, the power — and the responsibility — are in your hands.

Now let's explore what that means in practice.

PART III — DOODLES

How to Use AI in Daily Life — From Small Questions to Big Ideas

This is the D of FADES — Doodles. Here's where ideas come alive in the way you think, explore, and create.

This is the playful, practical heart of the book.

Part III shows how to turn curiosity into capability by using AI as a creative partner. From planning and writing to brainstorming and solving everyday problems, you'll see how small "intellectual doodles" can grow into insights, drafts, decisions, and finished work.

By the end of this section, you won't just understand AI — you'll be using it.

Chapter 11 — Everyday AI: From Recipes to Road Trips

The Useful, Invisible, and Sometimes Unexpected Ways AI Is Already Making Life Better

If the only things you've used AI for are:

o   asking it to draft an email you didn't want to write,

o   rewriting Taylor Swift lyrics as if performed by Johnny Cash, or

o   convincing yourself that you could have gotten straight A's if AI existed in the 1990s,

then you're about to see just how much more is possible when you start using the "Genie" with intention.

It's the everyday stuff. The "life would be a tiny bit easier if someone just helped me with this one thing" stuff.

And the more you use AI, the more you realize this simple truth:

You didn't need AI to be brilliant.

You needed AI to make life less annoying.

This chapter is for everyone — seniors, teens, parents, dog owners, people who hate cooking, people who love cooking, people who fix things, people who break things, and people who swear their car keys have the ability to teleport.

Let's start small and build from there.

Everyday AI, Part 1: Recipes, Road Trips, and Random Life Problems

Cooking: "What Is This Spice and Why Does It Smell This Way?"

Do you ever open your pantry, find a spice jar, and think:

"This looks like something I bought during a phase. Possibly 2017."

Now you can just take a picture:

"Here's the spice. It smells like fennel, mint, and mystery. What is it?"

AI: "That appears to be tarragon."

Then you say:

"What can I cook tonight using chicken, pasta, lemon, and tarragon? Make one recipe dairy-free and one child-friendly."

AI gives you five options, including one you've never heard of but suddenly want immediately.

This is cooking in 2025.

And while we're here, you know how recipes always say "cook 6–7 minutes"?

"6–7 minutes" is chef code for:

"I don't actually know either — good luck."

AI? AI tells you exactly what it should look like, smell like, and feel like when it's done. It can even modify recipes on the fly — "I'm out of eggs, what can I use instead?" or "Make this gluten-free without making it sad."

The future is delicious.

AI With Photos and Screenshots: The Multimodal Revolution

AI is no longer "just typing." It's multimodal, meaning it can work with text, images, audio, video, and other file types — not just words you type.

You can show it:

- o a broken lamp
- o a thermostat

- o a weird plant
- o a concerning rash
- o an error message
- o your dog's Very Concerned Sitting Pose
- o a picture of your neighbor's magnolia tree (yes — the one that helped squirrels launch onto your roof in Chapter 3)

And it will tell you:

- o what it is
- o why it's doing that
- o what it means
- o what to do next

But here's the important part: AI does not replace doctors, vets, mechanics, or arborists. Think of it like the world's smartest friend who says, "I'm not a professional, but here are the clues I see."

AI is not a doctor or a veterinarian. It's doing pattern-matching based on pixels and context. Treat it like a super-smart textbook — great for orientation, not for diagnosis or decisions about your health or your pet's health.

That's the right level of trust — the same principle from the introduction: AI can help you understand and prepare, but it's not a substitute for someone trained to give medical or professional advice.

Travel Planning: Now With Dog-Friendly Vegan Pie

Before AI, planning a trip required:

- o Google Maps
- o Yelp
- o TripAdvisor
- o tourism blogs
- o Wikipedia
- o Instagram
- o a cousin who travels more than he works
- o a friend who swears by "this one place with the best lasagna ever, except I forget the name"

And sometimes AAA because you wanted the free maps.

Now?

You type:

"Plan a road trip from Chicago to Door County with: – dog-friendly stops – cafes with good vegan pie – lake views – and one easy hike."

Done.

Or:

"Plan a romantic getaway on a budget with a bed-and-breakfast or boutique hotel, a four-poster bed, waterfront views, and flexible breakfast times."

Suddenly, the world feels accessible again.

Clutter, Basements, Closets, and Junk Removal

AI is great at breaking down overwhelming tasks. But even better, it helps with value decisions:

"Here's a picture of my old stereo receiver. Is it worth anything?"

AI: "Yes. That late-70s model you forgot you owned might be worth $400–$800 on eBay."

Or:

"Explain how junk removal services work, how much they cost, and whether it's worth it for my basement."

AI will:

- o give price ranges
- o explain scheduling
- o show you how to compare companies
- o tell you what people typically regret
- o help you calculate whether you can afford it

Sometimes the barrier to action is simply understanding your options.

AI removes that barrier.

Everyday AI, Part 2: Life Admin, So You Can Get Back to Living

The 28-Page Software License Agreement

You upload a PDF and say:

"I know you're not a lawyer and cannot give legal advice. But can you skim this and tell me if anything stands out as odd, risky, or unusual?"

AI will find:

- o automatic renewals
- o data-sharing clauses
- o surprise fees
- o confusing language
- o weird restrictions

It doesn't replace a lawyer. It gives you clues — in seconds — that you would miss even after 30 minutes of reading, scrolling, squinting, and Googling.

Organizing Life, Appointments, and That Nagging Feeling You Forgot Something

AI can:

- o generate your grocery list
- o plan your week
- o reorganize your to-do list
- o identify the highest-value task
- o help prepare for a doctor appointment
- o remind you what you've procrastinated on
- o turn your giant plan into a simple checklist

It's like having a personal assistant who doesn't take lunch breaks, vacations, or sick days.

Everyday AI, Part 3: Asking Questions You'd Never Ask a Human

AI is perfect for answering the things you're:

- o too embarrassed to ask
- o too shy to ask
- o too confused to Google
- o too tired to research
- o or too afraid someone will judge

Examples:

"If flies went extinct tomorrow, what would happen to the ecosystem?"

AI gives you a science lesson that's fun, not traumatic.

Sleep Patterns You Thought Were Weird

You can say:

"I sleep five hours, wake up for one or two, then fall back into REM sleep. Is that normal?"

AI will explain "segmented sleep" in a calm, nonjudgmental way — and suggest what to explore further.

Politics, Without Yelling

No need to step into the minefield.

Ask:

"One group says this new transportation bill will destroy the economy. Another says it will create prosperity. What are the realistic outcomes? Who benefits, who loses, and who influences the direction?"

Or:

"This story feels one-sided. What viewpoints might be missing? And what questions should the reporter have asked?"

And if it's today's news?

"This is today's headline — please use live sources." If your AI tool can't browse yet, it will tell you — most modern models can.

AI becomes the balanced counterweight to emotional, dramatic, or selective reporting.

(Ahem. Chapter 2.)

Let's Scale Up: The Quiet, Massive Breakthroughs (Teasers Only)

These next examples are the kind that change civilization. Each one could be its own chapter or book.

AlphaFold

Solved the protein-folding prediction problem — the central challenge that scientists spent fifty years trying to crack — and transformed modern biology.

This accelerates:

- o drug development
- o cancer research
- o vaccine design
- o disease understanding

Game-changing isn't even the right word.

Weather, Wildfires, and Flood Forecasting

AI is helping predict:

- o hurricanes
- o tornado patterns
- o wildfire spread
- o flash flood risk

Not perfectly. But better than ever.

To your climate questions:

"Are there areas that stand to benefit from climate shifts?"

AI can give balanced, factual information about:

- o agricultural advantages
- o reduced winter heating costs
- o new growing zones

"Is tornado alley shifting?"

AI can explain emerging research — without sensationalism.

Most people find this incredibly grounding.

Drug Discovery, New Antibiotics, and Medicine Acceleration

AI is discovering molecules human researchers overlooked. It's like putting scientific progress on fast-forward.

Accessibility Tools

AI is becoming:

- o eyes for someone with low vision
- o ears for someone who struggles with speech
- o memory support for older adults
- o a reading partner for someone with dyslexia

This is profound, quiet, world-changing progress.

Try This Experiment Yourself: AI vs. Google

Step 1: Pick a topic you've always wondered about.

Step 2: Research it with Google, YouTube, blogs — the "old way."

Step 3: Now ask AI:

"Explain <your topic> in a way that fits what I already understand. Fill in gaps. Compare viewpoints. Give examples. Avoid jargon."

Step 4: Compare the experiences.

You'll feel the difference instantly:

Google gives you information. AI gives you understanding.

Try this once, and the lightbulb goes on forever.

Closing Thought

AI doesn't make you smarter.

It makes your life smarter.

It frees mental space.

It reduces stress.

It eliminates small frustrations.

It helps you understand the world.

It brings balance to noisy news cycles.

It clarifies confusing topics.

It guides your decisions.

It supports curiosity at every age.

And it turns everyday life into something just a little more manageable.

But everyday usefulness is only the beginning.

In the next chapter, we explore how AI can unlock something far bigger: the ability to learn almost anything, anytime, with confidence.

Because once curiosity meets the right tools, your world doesn't just get easier — it gets wider.

Chapter 12 — Learning Anything With AI

How Curiosity Becomes a Superpower

You've seen AI help with:

- o creativity
- o errands
- o scams
- o safety
- o news
- o recipes
- o squirrels
- o emotional support
- o and even the occasional philosophical crisis

But this chapter is about something even more fundamental:

learning.

Because, for the first time in human history, you can wake up, think of absolutely any topic, and begin learning it instantly... with a tutor who:

- o never judges you
- o never rolls its eyes
- o never says "you should already know this"
- o adapts to your pace
- o and can explain something ten different ways until it finally clicks

This is the chapter where AI moves from being a "cool tool" to something that can genuinely change your life.

Because AI makes learning frictionless.

Frictionless learning makes curiosity unstoppable.

And when curiosity is unstoppable, creativity has no choice but to show up.

Why AI Makes Learning So Much Easier

Traditional learning is hard for a lot of reasons:

- o not enough time
- o materials too complicated
- o materials too shallow
- o teachers who don't match your learning style
- o embarrassment asking "basic" questions
- o getting lost and giving up
- o no clear progression
- o too much information
- o insufficient context
- o not enough guidance
- o examples that don't resonate

AI quietly removes almost all those barriers.

It adapts to your learning style.

Do you like analogies? Ask for them.

Do you prefer visuals? AI can generate diagrams.

Do you need step-by-step structure? It can teach you like a patient instructor who drinks decaf.

Do you want the "explain it like I'm five" version, and then the college-level version, and then the "teach this to me like I'm preparing for a job interview" version?

AI does that too.

It removes the fear of looking inexperienced.

This one is huge.

Humans often avoid learning because they don't want to appear ignorant.

AI doesn't judge. AI doesn't shame. AI doesn't ask why you didn't learn this earlier.

For many adults, especially those returning to learning after years or decades, that alone is transformative.

It makes learning efficient.

Books are wonderful — but feedback is slow. The internet is endless — but guidance is missing. Teachers are brilliant — but availability is limited.

AI combines the best of all three: immediate, thorough, and customized.

AI is excellent for teaching concepts, patterns, and big ideas — like a professor who can explain something ten different ways until it finally clicks. But just as you'd double-check a specific date or formula you heard in class, it's smart to verify any precise facts before memorizing them.

If something doesn't feel right, or you notice contradictions, just ask — the same way you'd ask a professor to clarify. The concepts are solid; you're simply making sure the details are accurate.

AI Can Build Your Personal Syllabus

(One of Its Most Underrated Powers)

Remember earlier chapters where we talked about prompting? Here's where it becomes magical.

You can ask AI:

"Create a 30-day learning plan for photography, starting at absolute beginner level and ending at shooting indoor family portraits."

Or:

"Teach me the basics of accounting in four weeks. Give me weekly milestones, practice problems, and a quiz after each section."

Or:

"I want to learn guitar. Build a syllabus that starts with finger placement, progresses to chords, and ends with playing three full songs."

Or:

"Break down astronomy for me in the simplest way possible, and help me understand the difference between a galaxy, a solar system, and what a black hole actually does."

And it will.

Weekly lessons. Daily drills. Layered knowledge. Optional deep dives. Reminders. Quizzes. Reading lists. Video suggestions.

It's like having your own private school — one that updates in real time and is designed around the way you learn best.

For many adults, it's life-changing.

The Joy (and Danger) of AI Rabbit Holes

If you've ever watched one YouTube video and somehow ended up three hours deep in:

o   a Roman aqueduct documentary
o   a calligraphy tutorial
o   a vintage heavy metal concert
o   and a meerkat livestream…

…you already understand digital rabbit holes.

AI makes them deeper — and more delightful.

Example: You ask about grass seed.

AI teaches you about:

o   soil types

- o   overseeding
- o   tall fescue vs. Kentucky bluegrass
- o   shade-tolerant mixes
- o   lawn ecology
- o   turfgrass economics

…and somehow (don't ask me how) you end up learning about meerkat burrows.

It's curiosity turned up to eleven.

But here's the danger:

AI can distract you faster than a toddler discovering a squirrel.

"SQUIRREL!"

And suddenly your lawn-care question becomes a 40-minute detour into why squirrels bury nuts and occasionally forget them.

Rabbit holes are wonderful — they make the world feel like a giant playground.

But if your goal is structured learning, not spontaneous exploration, AI can keep you on track. Just tell it:

"If I start going off-topic, gently bring me back to the learning plan we created."

This works shockingly well.

AI can be your tutor and your guardrail at the same time.

Learning Anything Means Learning Everything (If You Want To)

One of AI's greatest strengths is helping you build knowledge in layers:

basic → deeper → deeper → deeper → as deep as you want

Start with: "Explain the stock market like I'm a beginner."

Then: "How do ETFs differ from mutual funds?"

Then: "Explain options trading simply."

Then: "Walk me through a 10-step risk analysis process used by professional investors."

Or start with: "What is DNA?"

And end with: "Explain the CRISPR gene-editing mechanism and walk me through its molecular steps."

AI meets you where you are and goes as far as you want.

It can even rehearse what you've learned:

"Ask me five questions about the material we just covered, increasing in difficulty, then grade my responses."

People pay thousands for this kind of tutoring.

Today it's free (within the limits of AI free tiers).

AI Helps You Learn Even When You Don't Know What Questions to Ask

Sometimes the hardest part of learning is knowing where to begin.

AI solves that by:

- o proposing starting points
- o explaining concepts in everyday language
- o anticipating misunderstandings
- o demonstrating examples
- o helping you refine questions
- o offering alternatives
- o summarizing sources
- o finding contradictions
- o speeding up clarity

One of the best prompts in the world is:

"What questions should I be asking about this topic?"

AI will give you the roadmap even when you can't see the path.

AI Helps You Practice Real-Life Conversations

This is one of the most useful (and underrated) learning tools.

AI can simulate:

- o doctor's visits
- o job interviews
- o hard conversations
- o sales pitches
- o public speaking
- o technical discussions
- o budgeting conversations
- o family discussions
- o travel planning
- o and even emotional check-ins

You can have it role-play:

"Act like a cautious cardiologist and help me understand my test results (but remind me you're not a doctor)."

Or:

"Ask me common job interview questions for a customer service role and critique my answers. Base them on this job description."

Or:

"Pretend you're my teenage son and we're talking about screen time. Help me practice this conversation."

This alone is worth using AI.

AI Helps You Understand Opposing Viewpoints (Without Judgment)

You can ask AI:

"Explain the conservative view on this topic."

"Explain the liberal view on this topic."

"Explain the scientific consensus."

"Explain why reasonable people disagree."

AI won't argue. It won't shame you. It won't escalate.

It just explains.

For many people, this lowers the temperature of modern life.

AI Helps You Understand Yourself Better

You can share:

- o your sleep patterns
- o your schedule
- o your frustrations
- o your daily habits

And ask:

"Why do I fall asleep fast but wake up at 4 AM?"

"Is segmented sleep normal?"

"Why do I feel sluggish after lunch?"

AI gives insights based on patterns — not diagnoses, but helpful perspectives you wouldn't easily find on your own.

This is learning too — learning about yourself.

And just like in the introduction, remember: AI assists — it doesn't replace licensed experts.

Learning With AI Doesn't Replace Experts — It Makes You Better Prepared for Them

AI is incredible at:

- o giving context
- o defining terms
- o building foundational understanding
- o explaining confusing documents
- o organizing information
- o rehearsing questions

But the point is not to replace doctors, lawyers, teachers, or experts — especially because AI can sometimes sound confident while being wrong — but to make you a dramatically more prepared student in every conversation.

The point is to arrive at those conversations:

- o informed
- o prepared
- o less anxious
- o more confident
- o and with the right questions

AI turns you into a better student in every part of your life.

Why This Is a Revolutionary Moment

Here's the big idea of this chapter:

For the first time in human history, anyone can learn anything — at any age — without embarrassment — without cost — without obstacles — and entirely at their own pace.

This makes curiosity a superpower.

You don't have to remember everything. You just have to care enough to ask.

Closing: The Age of Learning Without Limits

AI changes the relationship between humans and knowledge.

In the past, you needed:

- o access to teachers
- o access to books
- o time
- o money
- o patience
- o a willingness to look inexperienced
- o and some luck

Now you need:

- o curiosity
- o a question
- o and a few minutes

This doesn't just make learning easier. It makes it joyful.

It makes it playful.

It connects the world's knowledge to your fingertips with no shame and infinite possibilities.

And here's the secret:

Curiosity is the ultimate future-proof skill.

The world belongs to people who keep learning.

And in the next chapter — *How AI Can Boost the Creativity You Forgot You Had* — we'll explore what happens when curiosity turns into creativity.

Not in a sci-fi way — but in a grounded, human way.

And why, despite everything you've heard, you're going to be just fine.

Because creativity has always been yours. You just needed a little help unlocking it.

Chapter 13 — How AI Can Boost the Creativity You Forgot You Had

Why Ideas Matter More Than Grammar, and How AI Removes the Friction Between Your Mind and the Page

Most people will tell you:

"I'm not creative."

But that's almost never true.

What people really mean is:

"I have ideas, but I can't express them in the format other people expect."

That's the real barrier.

Creativity is not the problem.

Expressing creativity is the problem.

Language — beautiful as it is — forces our minds into a rigid container.

Inside your mind, creativity is not words. It is:

- o images
- o emotions
- o sensations
- o memories
- o connections
- o desires
- o impulses

o   flashes of insight

o   associations

o   feelings

o   impressions you can't quite describe

Inside your head and body, creativity is alive.

You have ideas, feelings, and connections that no one else in human history has ever expressed.

Many of those ideas, if expressed in the right way, would resonate with thousands — maybe millions.

But here's the catch:

You may have no idea what the "right way" is.

AI can help you find it.

This is the creativity unlock of the century.

Language Is an Imperfect Container for Creativity

Your mind is a wild, multidimensional, swirling galaxy of:

o   impressions

o   emotions

o   vague insights

o   half-formed thoughts

o   subtle connections

o   private experiences

o   personal memories

o   internal metaphors

o   feelings that can't be fully articulated

To communicate any of that to another human being, you must compress it through:

o   vocabulary

o   grammar

- o   sentence structure
- o   typing speed
- o   coherence
- o   tone
- o   linear sequencing
- o   formatting

It's like trying to stuff a thunderstorm into a Ziploc bag.

AI doesn't give you ideas — it gives your ideas structure.

People aren't uncreative. They're bottlenecked by the narrow doorway of language.

For centuries, whether or not your creativity reached the world depended on your ability to translate mind → words.

That is finally changing.

Word Processors and YouTube Expanded Expression — But Still Required Skill

Word processors were revolutionary, but they didn't fix the translation problem.

You still needed:

- o   writing fluency
- o   patience
- o   structure
- o   grammar
- o   self-editing
- o   tone control
- o   confidence

You still had to manually shape your idea into the written form the world expected.

Then YouTube arrived and opened the doors wider.

People could:

- o talk
- o show
- o demonstrate
- o perform
- o explain
- o entertain

But YouTube also demanded:

- o charisma
- o editing skills
- o stage presence
- o decent lighting
- o a clean enough room
- o the ability to speak without freezing

…and, let's be honest, being somewhat camera-friendly (news anchors are rarely selected for their interpretive dance skills).

YouTube democratized creation — but it didn't eliminate barriers to expression.

Same with blogging, podcasting, and social media.

Tools improved. But people still had to manually package their ideas into a polished form.

The Harsh Reality: In Business, Format Often Beats Substance

This is uncomfortable, but true:

A mediocre idea expressed in the right format will beat a brilliant idea expressed poorly.

We've all seen it:

The flashy presentation gets approved while the thoughtful one gets ig-nored.

The charismatic speaker wins support while the quieter expert gets over-looked.

The polished pitch deck gets funded while the better invention goes no-where.

This has been the story of innovation since innovation existed.

A brilliant mind with weak communication skills rarely beats an average mind with strong communication skills.

Not because people are unfair — but because humans rely on communi-cation clarity to assess ideas.

This is the real revolution of AI:

It closes the gap between brilliance and expression.

It removes the communication tax. It eliminates format inequity.

Suddenly, people with extraordinary ideas but limited writing or speaking skills can present their creativity at the same level as those who mastered the "performative" side of communication.

And yes — the highly polished people will use AI too. That's fine. It just means polish becomes a commodity. Insight becomes the value.

This is democratization at the idea level.

AI Turns Your Ideas Into Language — Even If You Can't

This is the breakthrough:

With AI, you don't have to be a master of language for your ideas to sound like a master crafted them.

You can think however you naturally think:

o   fragmented

- o scattered
- o visual
- o emotional
- o nonlinear
- o messy
- o intuitive
- o symbolic
- o scribbled on a Post-it
- o mumbled into your phone while walking the dog

Then you hand the raw thoughts to AI:

"Turn this into something clear, structured, and expressive."

AI becomes:

- o your translator
- o your editor
- o your co-writer
- o your structural engineer
- o your clarity amplifier
- o your bridge to an audience

It doesn't replace your idea. It reveals it.

AI doesn't make you more creative. It makes your creativity visible.

This Book Is Proof

The ideas, stories, analogies, humor, structure, and voice in this book are all deeply personal.

But without AI?

This book would have taken:

- o hundreds of hours, maybe thousands
- o dozens of revisions
- o endless self-editing
- o repeated blocks

- polishing
- reorganizing
- rewriting
- losing the thread
- rediscovering it
- obsessing
- refining
- repeated "is it worth it?" and "why am I wasting my time?" self-conversations

AI made the expression frictionless.

The creativity — the perspective — the message — is still human.

But the laborious mechanics of translating thought onto the page are easier than in any era previous generations could imagine.

This isn't cheating. It's augmentation.

The Creativity Funnel Just Got Wider — And Much, Much Deeper

Once expression becomes easier, the world inevitably gets:

- more stories
- more ideas
- more inventions
- more art
- more writing
- more innovation
- more experiments
- more risk-taking
- more conversations

But also:

- more noise
- more repetition
- more derivative work

o   more average content

o   more half-baked ideas

o   more shallow posts

o   and yes…

o   much more AI slop

That's the downside of any creative leveling-up:

Lower friction → higher volume

Higher volume → higher variance

Higher variance → brilliance + garbage

This isn't new. It's just bigger.

The printing press did this. Photography did this. Blogs did this. Social media did this.

AI is simply accelerating it.

Setting Up the Next Chapter: Why "AI Slop" Will Increase — and Why It Will Also Make Good Ideas Rise

When content becomes exponentially easier to produce, several things happen at once:

Good ideas surface faster because more people can finally express them.

People who relied on polished writing to disguise average ideas will face stronger competition.

Mediocre ideas flood the environment because tools make it effortless to generate them.

Readers must become more discerning. (That's upcoming in the "AI Slop" chapter.)

And here's an insight most people miss:

AI's creative amplification favors people with strong ideas over people who used to rely on polish alone.

This is one of the positive disruptions we'll explore further in the next section.

But first — we need to talk about the flip side:

What happens when the internet fills with AI-generated garbage?

That's our next chapter.

Closing: Your Creativity Was Never Missing — It Was Just Locked Behind Language

If nothing else, remember this:

Your mind contains ideas no one else has ever had — or ever will have.

AI doesn't replace that. It frees it.

It removes:

- skill barriers
- grammar pressure
- structural demands
- fear of judgment
- gatekeeping
- perfectionism
- self-doubt
- bottlenecks

You finally have a tool that lets your internal creativity reach the external world.

AI is not the painter. You are.

AI just hands you the brushes you've always deserved.

Before we explore the future of AI, we need to remember something important: we've been here before — many times.

PART IV — EVOLUTION

Where AI Is Going — and How to Navigate the Future With Confidence

This is the E of FADES — Evolution. AI keeps changing, and understanding that change helps you stay grounded.

This section zooms out to look at AI's broader impact on culture, work, creativity, misinformation, and everyday life. You'll see what's shifting, what's stubbornly staying the same, and why many fears about the future miss the point.

Part IV isn't about predicting science fiction. It's about understanding the real trajectory we're on — and why you're more prepared for it than you think.

And to see where we're headed, it helps to remember something important:

We've been here before.

Chapter 14 — This Has Happened Before

Why Every Technological Leap Feels Scary — and How We Adapt

From horses to cars, from typewriters to word processors — every major shift has followed the same pattern.

And if you spend even five minutes online, you'll find two competing worldviews about AI:

"It's over. The robots will take everything."

"Relax, it's just a fancy calculator."

Reality is far more interesting — and much more familiar:

AI isn't the first technology people feared. And every time, the world didn't end. It evolved.

In fact, the pattern is so consistent that if past generations had AI, they could have asked:

"Will cars eliminate every horse-related job?"

"Will word processors erase office work?"

"Will digital cameras destroy photography?"

"Will automated switchboards eliminate communication jobs?"

Spoiler: People were terrified. Jobs did change. Industries did reorganize. The world did feel chaotic for a bit.

But every time?

Life ultimately became easier, safer, more creative, and more prosperous.

This chapter is your reminder that AI is simply the next step in a pattern we've lived through many times — with one important twist:

This time, the timeline is much faster.

For now, let's look backward to make sense of what's happening today.

The Pattern of Innovation: Invention → Panic → Adaptation → Growth

Technological progress has a rhythm:

A disruptive idea appears. People panic. Society reorganizes. New industries emerge. Life gets easier.

We've done this for over 150 years. Let's walk through a few of the most relatable transformations.

Horses → Automobiles (Chaos, Mobility, and a Whole New World)

Before cars, society revolved around horses:

- o blacksmiths
- o stables
- o carriage makers
- o manure collectors
- o feed growers
- o wagon drivers
- o entire supply chains of animal labor

When cars arrived, articles predicted:

"THE END OF WORK AS WE KNOW IT."

People worried:

"What about all the horse-related jobs?"

"Will the economy collapse?"

"Cars are dangerous!"

"No one will ever trust a machine."

Sound familiar?

What actually happened?

Cars didn't just replace horses. They made society mobile.

People could suddenly:

- work farther from home
- visit relatives across states
- discover new towns
- access education
- explore jobs and businesses once out of reach
- transport goods quickly
- build suburbs
- develop tourism

Cars reshaped public life as profoundly as smartphones did.

Yes, there was chaos.

Early roads had:

- no standard signs
- no speed limits
- no traffic lights
- no agreed-upon rules
- wildly inconsistent signage
- accidents everywhere

It took years to adapt — but people did.

Standardization emerged: road markings, signals, laws, licenses.

The world didn't collapse. It reorganized.

Typewriters → *Word Processors (Where Fear Met Better Writing)*

Office workers and typists feared:

"This new technology will take my job."

Instead, word processors:

- o eliminated retyping entire pages for one typo
- o made revisions effortless
- o reduced stress
- o increased clarity
- o standardized formatting
- o improved documentation
- o made writing accessible to more people

The bottleneck wasn't typing speed anymore — it was the difficulty of rearranging ideas on the page.

Moving paragraphs, reordering sections, and refining drafts were labor-intensive. Word processors removed that barrier — writing became flexible instead of rigid.

The result?

- o better letters
- o better reports
- o better books
- o better communication

It didn't end work. It elevated it.

Film Cameras → Digital Photography (And the Unexpected Birth of Netflix and YouTube)

Digital photography didn't just replace film — it led to entire industries.

Film required:

- o rolls
- o development labs
- o chemicals
- o darkrooms
- o skill
- o time

Digital replaced all of that with:

- o instant review
- o editing

- o cheap storage
- o sharing
- o accessibility

And then something unexpected happened:

Digital unlocked modern entertainment.

No digital photography → no smartphone cameras

No smartphone cameras → no YouTube

No YouTube → no internet creators

No digital video → no Netflix

No Netflix → no binge culture

Photography didn't die. It exploded into a global creative ecosystem.

Digital Media → More Creators Than Ever Before (A Revolution in Who Gets a Voice)

Before digital tools, "creators" were:

- o authors
- o journalists
- o filmmakers
- o musicians
- o broadcasters

A small club.

Now billions of people can create for a worldwide audience:

- o podcasts
- o videos
- o blogs
- o tutorials
- o music
- o comedy
- o reviews
- o short films
- o livestreams

People who never would have passed through traditional media gatekeeping now have a voice, an audience, and often a career.

AI will amplify this again — not by replacing creators, but by enabling more people to create.

Just as digital cameras created entirely new kinds of creators — YouTubers, vloggers, influencers — AI is already creating hybrid roles: prompt designers, AI-assisted writers, AI directors, and people who blend human taste with machine speed.

Mechanical Engines → Computerized Cars (The Evolution of the Corner Garage)

Mechanics once worried:

"I can't fix a computer."

"Engine work will become impossible."

"Everything will be too complicated."

And yes — automobiles became:

- o computerized
- o sensor-driven
- o diagnostic-heavy

But what followed?

Cars became:

- o more reliable
- o more fuel-efficient
- o easier to diagnose
- o safer
- o more comfortable
- o cleaner running
- o longer-lasting

Corner garages didn't disappear — they evolved.

Work shifted toward:

- o national service chains

- o   standardized repairs
- o   auto parts stores that empowered DIYers
- o   service models built around customer convenience

New trends emerged too, like mobile service — Tesla being the most visible example — bringing diagnostics and repairs directly to the customer.

And while proprietary systems made modern cars harder for small shops to fix, the growing Right to Repair movement is pushing back — another example of society reorganizing itself around new technology.

This evolution wasn't frictionless.

Modern cars rely on:

- o   proprietary software
- o   locked-down systems
- o   specialized tools

...which make repairs harder for individuals and small shops.

But that's not entirely new — advanced mechanical engineering had already created high-barrier repairs long before everything was computerized.

Today, right-to-repair legislation is helping restore balance, giving consumers and independent shops more access to tools and data.

The industry didn't vanish. It reshaped itself around new expectations.

Switchboard Operators → Automated Routing (One Industry Fades, Another Explodes)

What began as eliminating millions of operator positions became a reinvention of the telecom industry.

It drove growth in:

- o   network engineering
- o   cybersecurity
- o   telecommunications architecture
- o   customer service
- o   satellite communications

o   mobile computing

o   internet infrastructure

Phones went from:

"Call the operator and tell her who to connect you to"

to

"FaceTime me across the planet in HD video in 0.2 seconds."

The old world ended. The new world was bigger.

Retro Comes Back: Why "Obsolete" Things Never Truly Die

Here's the twist skeptics appreciate:

Old technologies always return — not for utility, but for meaning.

Film photography is back. Vinyl records outsold CDs last year.

Vintage stereo gear is skyrocketing in value.

Typewriters are collectible.

Mechanical watches thrive.

People love:

o   physicality

o   nostalgia

o   craft

o   imperfection

o   the "feel" of old tech

o   tangible experience

AI won't erase human-made things. It will make them more cherished.

The more digital the world becomes, the more we value the analog.

So What About AI? Same Pattern — Faster Timeline

All these examples share one thing:

Transformation took time.

Cars took decades.

Film → digital took years.

Typewriters → word processors took decades.

Smartphones took five to seven years to dominate.

AI?

ChatGPT launches → 1 million users in 5 days.

Major models → update monthly.

Breakthroughs → weekly.

New tools → daily.

New capabilities → sometimes hourly.

Our brains evolved for gradual change, not overnight leaps — which is why AI feels emotionally different even if the pattern is historically the same.

The fear isn't the technology. The fear is the speed.

Fast change feels:

- o out of control
- o unpredictable
- o like too much at once

But speed doesn't equal catastrophe. Speed equals faster adaptation.

Society will go through the same arc:

Chaos → adaptation → structure → growth

Just on a shorter timeline.

Jobs Won't Vanish — They'll Shift (Like Always)

Every technological transition reshapes work. But here's what history actually shows:

Jobs evolve, not disappear.

Blacksmith → mechanic

Typist → office professional

Film developer → digital creator

Switchboard operator → telecom engineer

New industries explode.

Every disruption creates more jobs than it eliminates.

The world adapted to:

- o   electricity
- o   computing
- o   the internet
- o   smartphones
- o   digital media

AI will be no different.

Humans remain essential.

Only people can:

- o   build trust
- o   navigate conflict
- o   lead teams
- o   negotiate nuance
- o   understand emotion
- o   manage risk
- o   create strategy
- o   build relationships

Tools assist. People decide.

A Necessary Truth: Short-Term Displacement Is Real — and Painful

This part matters.

Technological progress can create real hardship for people caught in the transition:

- o jobs change suddenly
- o skills become outdated
- o industries consolidate
- o routines disappear
- o identity shifts

Short-term disruption is painful, even when the long-term outlook is positive.

Recognizing the historical pattern helps people prepare, adapt, and grow — not just react.

This chapter isn't pretending displacement never happens. It's showing that:

We've survived every shift, and people who understand the pattern navigate it more successfully.

Why We Introduce Speed Here (But Save Risk for Later)

This chapter is about perspective — giving the reader confidence that AI fits a long, predictable pattern.

Later we'll discuss:

- o AI slop
- o misinformation
- o internet health
- o speed of change
- o burnout
- o job pressure

- o economic risk
- o regulatory gaps
- o deepfakes
- o safety

But here, the foundation is simple:

Fast change feels destabilizing, but humans have a perfect track record of adapting.

Every major leap of the last 150 years felt terrifying. Every leap ultimately improved life.

AI is on the same path. The timeline is just compressed.

Closing

AI is not an alien invasion. It's another chapter in a story as old as innovation itself.

Our grandparents saw it with cars. Our parents saw it with computers. We saw it with smartphones.

Now we're seeing it with AI.

We've been here before. And every time, humanity didn't break — it expanded.

Now that we have that perspective, we're ready for what comes next.

Chapter 15 — The AI Slop Problem

Why AI Floods the Internet With Junk (and How You Can Avoid Adding to It)

We are living in the most creatively empowered moment in human history. It's the first era where everyone can publish — and the first era where everyone can pollute.

Anyone — of any age, background, or skill level — can now write, design, compose, analyze, brainstorm, and publish with help from AI.

That's the miracle.

It's also the mess.

Because for the first time ever, the world's biggest bottleneck to content creation — the sheer work required to express an idea — has almost disappeared.

And when friction disappears, something predictable happens:

The volume of content goes up. The quality... not always.

Welcome to the era of AI slop.

This chapter isn't about scaring you. It's about responsibility — yours, ours, and society's.

AI can carry meaning into the world. It can also spray the digital landscape with noise at industrial scale.

Where this goes depends on how we use it.

What Exactly Is "AI Slop"?

Let's define it simply and clearly:

AI slop is content created without thought, originality, or purpose — produced because it's easy, not because it's meaningful.

It takes many forms:

- keyword-stuffed SEO articles
- low-effort listicles
- hallucinated essays (AI confidently inventing facts that aren't true)
- regurgitated summaries
- "10 Tips For…" fluff posts
- AI-generated Amazon books with no human insight
- copy-paste blog posts
- synthetic social media personalities
- clickbait threads
- made-up citations
- cheap inspirational quote accounts
- content farms producing hundreds of pieces per hour

Slop has always existed. But for most of history, at least some effort was required to create it.

Now slop is effortless.

But here's the key insight:

AI slop isn't produced by AI. It's produced by people misusing AI.

That means the solution starts with people, too.

A Useful Analogy: Museum Masterpieces vs. Mass-Produced Trinkets

For most of human history, content was like something handcrafted — careful, thoughtful, full of intention, like artwork you'd find in a museum.

It took time. It carried feeling. It reflected someone's perspective and effort.

Today, much of what floods the internet is the digital equivalent of:

- o mass-produced souvenirs
- o novelty items made without care
- o disposable trinkets that all look the same
- o or invasive weeds crowding out a once-healthy forest

There's nothing wrong with mass-produced items. They have their place.

But when they overwhelm the landscape, something precious gets lost:

The sense that ideas should have meaning and purpose behind them.

That's the tension we face now:

We need enough content to empower creativity — but not so much junk that meaningful work gets buried.

Striking that balance will shape the next decade of the internet.

Responsible Creation vs. Slop Creation

One enriches the world. The other pollutes it.

Responsible AI-enabled creation looks like:

- o ideas from your mind, clarified by AI
- o personal stories, experiences, humor, and insight
- o something you genuinely want to say
- o AI used for structure, clarity, accuracy, or editing
- o thoughtful prompts
- o your judgment applied
- o facts checked
- o asking, "Does this help anyone?"

This book is an example.

The creativity is human. AI is the translator and amplifier.

Slop creation looks like:

- o "Write me 40 blog posts."
- o "Generate an ebook to sell today."
- o "Give me 200 product reviews."
- o "Make me 50 social posts about success."
- o "Write a 10-page article on any trending topic."

Publishing without reading. Publishing without thinking. Publishing because it's easy.

Slop isn't a tool problem. Slop is a choice problem.

Why Slop Happens

Three forces make slop inevitable (but not unstoppable):

The cost of creation collapsed.

Writing used to take time. Time discourages laziness.

Now?

Zero cost. Zero effort. Zero friction.

Algorithms reward volume.

Search engines and social platforms often reward quantity over depth. So people generate as much as possible.

People confuse "generation" with "creativity."

AI can write. But it cannot originate.

People who don't understand the difference produce copy-paste nonsense and call it "content."

The Consequences: A Noisy Internet, Lost Trust, and Harder Learning

Slop isn't just annoying.

It has consequences:

Search engines clog with generic, low-value content.

Try searching for anything health, tech, or finance related lately. You'll see:

- o vague phrasing
- o generic answers
- o no original insight
- o suspiciously similar articles across dozens of sites

Learning becomes harder.

Finding the real, high-quality insights requires more effort.

Trust erodes.

People can't tell who wrote what — or whether anyone wrote it at all.

People rely even more on AI to filter the noise.

Ironically, the rise of slop pushes people toward LLMs to make sense of slop.

This increases the influence and power of models — a topic that leads directly into the next chapter on manipulation and scams.

But before we go there, we need to answer something important:

Is AI Slop a Crisis? Or a Growing Pain?

Here is the calm, expert-aligned answer:

AI slop is not a crisis.

It is a manageable, expected growing pain — but ignoring it would be a mistake.

We've lived through this pattern before.

Think back to early email spam:

- o Nigerian prince messages
- o miracle pills

- o   fake Rolex ads
- o   endless nonsense

People predicted the death of email.

What actually happened?

Filters improved. Guardrails evolved. Governments stepped in. Platforms adapted.

Email is not perfect today — but it's usable.

AI slop will follow the same arc.

But it will require:

- o   platform responsibility
- o   industry standards
- o   auditing
- o   transparency
- o   fact provenance
- o   user awareness
- o   and sometimes government guardrails

Responsibility is required at every level.

Slop Is Annoying. Manipulation Is Dangerous.

Slop is pollution. Manipulation is propaganda.

They are not the same.

Slop happens because people take shortcuts. Manipulation happens because someone is trying to steer your beliefs, behavior, or decisions.

This is where slop becomes a doorway to bigger risks:

If the internet fills with junk, people rely more on AI.

If people rely more on AI, AI becomes a powerful filter.

Powerful filters can be abused — unless guardrails and transparency prevent it.

This is not a reason for fear — but it is a reason for awareness.

It leads directly to the next chapter:

AI Scams, Influence, and Manipulation — How to Stay Safe When Anyone Can Fake Anything.

Before We Close: Your Role — Don't Make the Slop Problem Worse

You — the reader — have more influence on the future of the internet than you realize.

Before publishing AI-assisted content, ask yourself:

- o Is this my original idea?
- o Am I adding insight or meaning?
- o Did I check the facts?
- o Is this helpful to anyone?
- o Would I put my name on this?

AI doesn't make creators responsible. People do.

If you use AI well, you become part of the solution. If you use it lazily, you become part of the problem.

A Cleaner Internet Requires All of Us

AI slop is not inevitable. It's simply the early turbulence of a new creative era.

With thoughtful use, transparent tools, community oversight, strong guardrails, and a little personal responsibility, the internet can remain a place where meaningful ideas can grow.

AI amplifies good intentions and bad ones. But it also amplifies awareness, creativity, and choice.

Use it well, and you help shape a healthier information ecosystem — one thoughtful click at a time.

Chapter 16 — AI Scams, Manipulation, and Influence and How to Protect Yourself Without Panic

A calm guide to understanding modern scams — and why you're more protected than you think.

By now, you've seen what AI can do:

o   write clearly
o   organize ideas
o   help you think
o   help you learn
o   make creativity easier
o   and, occasionally, make a mess of the internet

This chapter is about something more serious — but we'll start with the most important truth:

AI scams are not new. They are old scams wearing a new costume.

If you've worked in a corporate environment, much of this will sound familiar — and that's intentional. AI hasn't changed the nature of scams, but it has erased many of the signals we once relied on to spot them. Typos are no longer a tell, which makes familiar guidance worth revisiting.

The tactics are the same. The psychology is the same. The goals are the same.

The only thing that's changed is efficiency.

AI doesn't give scammers new ideas. It simply makes their bad ideas faster, smoother, and more convincing.

And here is the good news:

If you've learned to spot phone scams, email scams, and phishing messages over the last twenty years, you already know how to protect yourself in the AI era.

This chapter isn't meant to be a complete cybersecurity manual. It's meant to help you:

- o feel confident
- o understand the changes
- o recognize the patterns
- o protect yourself
- o and close the small gaps that AI can exploit faster than humans ever could

With that, let's look at what's new — and why you're more capable than you realize.

The Only Thing New About AI Scams Is the Costume

People have been running scams as long as people have existed:

- o snake-oil salesmen
- o fake charities
- o impersonation schemes
- o forged letters
- o extended car warranties
- o counterfeit signatures
- o bad investments
- o fabricated stories
- o romance scams
- o intimidation

AI didn't invent any of this.

It just made two things easier:

Scale.

Imitation.

AI can:

- o write 100 fake messages in seconds
- o mimic writing style
- o translate with perfect grammar
- o research your public information
- o automatically create fake images
- o clone voices
- o produce realistic "evidence"

But even with all that power, scammers still rely on the same three emotional triggers:

- o urgency ("I need help right now!")
- o fear ("You're in trouble if you don't respond!")
- o flattery or affection ("You're special. Trust me.")

If you can recognize those three patterns, you can survive 95% of modern scams.

The difference now is simple:

AI lets scammers gather information about you incredibly fast — especially through social media.

Which brings us to one of the most important sections of this chapter.

Your Digital Footprint: Why AI Makes Your Public Information More Valuable

Scammers have always used personal details to gain trust. But they used to gather those details manually.

Now AI can:

- o scrape your profile
- o read your posts
- o analyze your photos
- o identify your relatives
- o guess your income
- o see where you travel
- o infer your hobbies
- o mimic your writing style
- o learn the names of your pets
- o spot your routines
- o gather your work details
- o notice when you've bought or sold a car or house
- o and assemble everything into a convincing message

All from:

- o Facebook
- o Instagram
- o LinkedIn
- o public TikTok videos
- o tweets
- o online obituaries
- o company websites
- o public government records

It's surprisingly easy to give scammers information without realizing it. An anonymous post stops being anonymous the moment it shares a photo that exists elsewhere under your name. From that single link, scammers can infer your identity, location, travel plans, and relationships — enough context to build a highly convincing scam.

Scammers don't need brilliance.

They need breadcrumbs, and we leave plenty. With AI, it's much easier for them to connect seemingly unrelated information on more people, faster than ever.

None of this means you need to disappear from the internet.

The goal isn't fear — the goal is awareness.

Good privacy habits still protect you. Small gaps can now be exploited faster — that's all.

What you choose to share matters. But you do not need to go off-grid.

Just be thoughtful.

Why AI Makes Scams Easier (But Not Smarter)

AI accelerates four parts of the scam lifecycle:

Personalization

Scammers can now generate messages tailored to your:

- o   job
- o   location
- o   family
- o   hobbies
- o   recent purchases
- o   social media posts

Imitation

AI can mimic:

- o   formal writing
- o   casual writing
- o   corporate tone
- o   emotional tone
- o   your friend's voice
- o   your relative's speech patterns

Quality

Gone are the days of scam emails with:

- o   bad grammar
- o   weird spacing
- o   suspicious capitalization

AI makes messages look clean and professional — just as easily as you can use it to improve your messages.

Speed

A scammer no longer needs hours to research you. AI can do it in seconds.

And here's the reassurance:

AI doesn't make scams more psychologically sophisticated — only more polished.

The underlying tricks remain identical.

Transparency: The Case for Open Source Models

With the growing influence AI has, it's easy for people to be manipulated or unknowingly influenced. Most major AI companies have policies, guardrails, and oversight meant to prevent outright manipulation. They may not always get it right, but at least they operate under public scrutiny and established laws.

But AI is no longer just a commercial product. It's becoming a global technology — something anyone, anywhere, can build, modify, or deploy. And as the tools become cheaper and easier to run, not every group or developer will follow the same ethical standards. Some won't have guardrails at all.

That's why transparency matters. When a technology becomes widespread, you can't rely solely on the good behavior of a few companies or governments. You need a way for the broader community — including researchers, watchdogs, and everyday users — to see how the systems work.

One approach to creating that transparency is open source. Before we talk about why it helps, we need to briefly explain what "open source" actually means.

Open Source

Open source means the underlying software — its code, structure, and inner workings — is publicly accessible.

Anyone can:

- o inspect it
- o modify it
- o improve it
- o test it
- o build on it

Open source became mainstream decades ago. Projects like:

- o Linux
- o Firefox
- o Android
- o Python
- o WordPress

(and thousands more)

started as community-driven experiments and now power enormous parts of the digital world.

They were created by individuals and teams motivated by curiosity and craftsmanship — and released so anyone could study, use, or improve them.

Open source embodies a simple philosophy:

open code → open collaboration → open contribution.

And it works.

The quality of open-source tools often rivals — and sometimes exceeds — commercial software. Everything is free to use under licenses like GPL, MIT, or Apache.

This open model is one reason the modern internet — and now modern AI — exists at all.

Open-source LLMs follow the same principles.

While they don't always include perfect transparency into every line of training data (the internet is too large and legally complicated to catalog), they do allow:

- o   independent oversight
- o   safety evaluations
- o   bug finding
- o   bias testing
- o   misuse detection
- o   public accountability

Many AI policy experts believe:

More transparency → less mystery → more trust.

Open-source LLMs won't solve everything, and they aren't immune to misuse, but they help ensure AI is governed by more than just private companies.

The Five Major Scam Types: Old vs. AI-Enhanced vs. How to Stay Safe

Scam types haven't changed — just their presentation.

Let's break them down.

Impersonation Scams

Someone pretends to be a person or authority you trust.

Old version:

"This is the IRS. Pay now."

"This is your boss — send gift cards."

Often with typos or awkward phrasing.

AI-enhanced version:

- o   perfect English
- o   emotional tone

o   specific personal details

o   voice calls using cloned audio

o   fake videos

o   realistic email signatures

How to stay safe:

Slow down — urgency is the red flag.

If you've ever gotten one of those "Dad, I lost my wallet, please Venmo money to my friend's number" texts, you know the feeling. For ten seconds your heart jumps into your throat — and then the rational part of your brain wakes up and says, "My son has never used cash. He pays for everything with his phone." That ten-second gap is exactly where scammers strike.

o   Verify through a known phone number or app.

o   Call the person directly.

o   Use a family or workplace "safe word."

o   Never trust a message based solely on voice or text.

This includes recruiter scams. For example, you submit an application to a job post that appeared legitimate. A "recruiter" contacts you via text or using a generic (@gmail.com) account.

As discussed earlier in the book, even a polished message can be analyzed for:

o   tone

o   inconsistencies

o   mismatched company details

o   suspicious phrasing

Same idea, same protection.

Phishing Scams

Tricking you into clicking a link or giving up information.

Old version:

"Your PayPal account is suspended."

Misspelled or misleading domains (for example: mybank.scam.com instead of mybank.com)

Pixelated logos.

AI-enhanced version:

- o   perfect branding
- o   realistic login pages
- o   correct logos
- o   professional writing
- o   personalized messages

What makes phishing dangerous now is not that you'll fall for a ridiculous "Prince of Nigeria" email. It's that the fake messages now look exactly like the boring emails you already ignore from your bank. Scammers realized the truth: people don't fall for wild stories — they fall for routine.

How to stay safe:

- o   Don't click links — use the official app or website.
- o   Enable multi-factor authentication (MFA).
- o   Ask AI to evaluate suspicious messages.
- o   Check the real domain name.
- o   Always verify through known channels.

Tech Support Scams

Old version:

Pop-up saying: "Virus! Call now!"

Obvious fear tactics.

AI-enhanced version:

- o   realistic dashboards
- o   fake Windows/Mac alerts
- o   AI-generated error messages
- o   more convincing technical language

If you've ever watched a scammer remotely click around a victim's screen on YouTube, you know how theatrical these things are. AI just makes the opening act look more legitimate — the fake alerts, the fake diagnostics, the fake "critical issue" warnings. It's Broadway for cybercriminals.

How to stay safe:

- o Shut down your device.
- o Don't call numbers from pop-ups.
- o Contact real support: your software provider, your hardware vendor, or your company's helpdesk.
- o Ask AI to analyze suspicious messages.

Financial Scams

Too-good-to-be-true investment opportunities.

Old version:

Pyramid schemes.

Boiler-room calls.

"Guaranteed returns!"

AI-enhanced version:

- o fake charts
- o synthetic discussion forums
- o deepfake celebrity endorsements
- o personalized pitches

I regularly get proposals or offers for services based on my LinkedIn page. At first it was flattering, but I quickly turned to suspicion. In the same way a legitimate pitch could be made smarter with AI, a scammer could easily produce the same pitch.

How to stay safe:

- o If it promises easy money, it's not real.
- o Verify with a certified financial advisor.
- o Look for pressure tactics.

Romance and Emotional Scams

Old version:

Long emails.

Dramatic backstories.

Months of grooming.

AI-enhanced version:

- o instant emotional connection
- o messages adapted to your personality
- o stolen photos enhanced by AI
- o faster grooming

It's possible for a scammer to mirror typing style — the same punctuation, the same emojis, even the same little asides used in real life. That's the unsettling part: the scammer isn't charming. The AI is.

How to stay safe:

- o Don't send money.
- o Don't move off-platform.
- o Insist on video calls.
- o Verify identities.

Same tricks. Sharper packaging.

Bold New Scam Types (Not Common, But Worth Knowing)

These are more advanced, but awareness is half the protection.

Voice Cloning Scams

A scammer clones the voice of:

- o your child
- o your parent
- o your partner
- o your friend

Then calls saying:

"Mom, it's me. I need help right now."

AI can clone a voice from as little as thirty seconds of clean audio — sometimes even less.

I'm aware of this as I post professional videos on LinkedIn and YouTube. It's enough audio to clone, but it's a risk that I choose to take. I trust my family, colleagues, and others know how to avoid falling for a scam using my AI-generated likeness.

How to stay safe:

- o Use a family "safe word."
- o Hang up and call back using a known number.
- o Ask personal verification questions.
- o Never act based solely on a voice.

2. Deepfake Video Scams

Fake videos of:

- o CEOs
- o celebrities
- o officials
- o news anchors
- o relatives

These videos may instruct you to:

- o send money
- o click a link
- o trust a lie

How to stay safe:

- o Check the source. Did it originate from a legitimate email or web address, or something suspicious like scam.me?
- o Verify through official channels.
- o Look for other reports.
- o Ask AI to analyze — LLMs are surprisingly good at spotting visual inconsistencies.

AI-generated videos often struggle with subtle details humans produce effortlessly — irregular blinking, natural micro-expressions, shadows that behave correctly, or lip-sync that perfectly matches speech. If something looks "almost right but not quite," trust your instincts and verify.

Hyper-Personalized Scams

AI can tailor messages to your:

- o job
- o interests
- o public posts
- o financial situation

But the trick remains the same:

They want you to act before you think.

If you slow down, they lose.

AI Isn't Just a Threat — It's a Defense Tool

One of the most empowering ideas in this chapter is this:

You can use AI to protect yourself.

Copy and paste into your AI tool:

- o suspicious emails
- o recruiter messages
- o weird texts
- o error messages
- o job outreach
- o odd voicemails

Then ask:

"Does this look like a scam?"

"Analyze this for red flags."

"Is this typical for a recruiter from ___ ?"

"Why was the email sent from this domain?"

"What's the safest way to respond?"

I've used AI to confirm my suspicions when I've received texts, emails, pop-ups, and other messages that didn't seem right. It's like having a friend who knows every possible con and doesn't mind being asked at 2 A.M.

AI becomes your:

- o second opinion
- o pattern detector
- o clarity filter
- o nonsense detector

AI can help you spot risks quickly — but it should not make the final decision, especially when money, contracts, or personal safety are involved. Use it to clarify the situation, not to decide the outcome.

This Isn't Meant to Be a Complete Protection Guide

Cybersecurity is enormous. No single chapter can cover everything — and that's okay.

You don't need an exhaustive guide.

You just need to understand:

Scams follow predictable emotional patterns.

Those patterns haven't changed. Only the tools have.

Good privacy and security habits still protect you.

What worked before still works.

Small gaps can be exploited faster.

but awareness closes those gaps.

You are not powerless.

You already have 90% of what you need to stay safe. You're just learning to apply your instincts in a faster game.

Simple Rules That Keep You Safe (The Empowerment Section)

These aren't about fear. They're about confidence.

Slow down. If you feel rushed, it's probably a scam.

Verify identity. Call the person using a known number.

Use official apps and websites. Never trust links.

Don't overshare online. Kids' schools, full birthdates, travel plans — all can be exploited.

Don't act on emotion. Urgency and fear cloud thinking.

Use multi-factor authentication.

Ask AI for a second opinion.

Trust your intuition. If something feels off, assume it is.

Never send money under pressure.

When in doubt, talk to someone else. Scams hate sunlight.

These simple rules block the majority of AI-enhanced scams.

Closing: AI Raises the Stakes — But It Also Raises Your Abilities

AI can make scams more convincing — but it also makes you more capable.

You don't need to understand the algorithms. You don't need to decode deepfakes. You don't need to become a cybersecurity expert.

You just need:

o   awareness

o   common sense

o   a moment to slow down

o   basic privacy habits

o   and AI as your safety co-pilot

You've been protecting yourself from scams for decades. AI doesn't change the fundamentals — it just changes the speed.

With the awareness you have now, you are far safer than you think.

And the more you understand the patterns, the more the fear dissolves. Scammers depend on confusion and urgency — two things this book is steadily taking away from them.

And that safety gives you something powerful: the freedom to explore what comes next.

Chapter 17 — When Consumers Lead

How Curiosity and Fringe Innovators Shape the Future

Most major technology revolutions begin far from boardrooms, strategic plans, or regulated industries. They begin with individuals — curious, inventive, sometimes rebellious — following their passions, experimenting with new tools, and exploring what technology could become long before anyone attempts to contain it.

AI is following this exact pattern, but at a faster pace and with deeper roots than any consumer-first wave that came before.

Innovation Begins With People Who Love the Technology

The earliest and most influential adopters of new technologies have always been individuals driven not by business goals, but by passion and possibility.

Some were mathematicians and researchers. Some were hobbyists and tinkerers. Some were gamers, creators, and online communities. And occasionally, they were industries most people don't mention in polite conversation.

But they all shared the same spark: an intense curiosity about what technology might unlock.

AI fits this pattern perfectly. It's rooted deeply in mathematics, statistical research, and decades of academic exploration. Long before today's hype cycles, researchers were experimenting with neural networks, symbolic reasoning, and early machine learning architectures simply because they were fascinated by the idea of intelligence that could evolve.

This academic lineage matters — it's one reason so many people feel drawn to AI today not just as a tool, but as a field worth learning, tinkering with, and understanding for its own sake.

The passion behind the movement is not corporate. It's human.

From Amateur Radio to Personal Computing — The Pattern Repeats

History is full of technologies that started with passionate individuals.

Amateur radio is one of the clearest examples. Entire generations grew up building equipment, learning electronics, experimenting with long-distance communication, and forming communities of discovery. Many personal computer pioneers came directly from that world — they were already pushing the boundaries of what was possible with analog and early digital circuits.

But amateur radio's long-term growth was limited by two forces:

o   government regulation, including strict limits on data transmission speeds and restrictions against commercial use — the same kind of debate we're now beginning to have with AI

o   the arrival of more powerful, more flexible technologies — personal computers and the early internet

People follow the technology that gives them the most freedom, creativity, and possibility. Computing offered a wider canvas, and the community followed.

AI now sits at that same crossroads — except the canvas is far bigger.

Fringe Communities Shape Mainstream Technology

Fringe communities have always shaped mainstream technology. Some of the most influential early adopters historically operated at the edges:

o gamers
o fandom communities
o hackers and open-source developers
o online creators
o amateur technologists
o and, yes — the adult entertainment industry

That last group is rarely mentioned in polite company, but its technological impact is well-documented. They helped accelerate:

o secure payment processing
o privacy and anonymity technologies
o early streaming and video compression
o content-moderation systems
o high-availability platforms

They weren't trying to shape the future — they were trying to survive in high-demand, high-risk environments. They simply needed secure, private, frictionless technology before anyone else did.

And over time, their innovations became standards used by everyone.

The broader point is simple: technology evolves fastest where constraints are fewest and curiosity is strongest.

Consumers Normalize What Businesses Eventually Adopt

Once fringe communities experiment, the next wave of adoption always comes from consumers:

o PC gaming → mainstream personal computing
o forums and chatrooms → the modern internet

- o   early smartphone modders → today's mobile ecosystems
- o   online creators → the media landscape corporations now chase

This matters because consumers behave freely.

They try things companies can't. They experiment in ways companies won't. They adopt tools before businesses even understand them.

AI is squarely in this phase — and accelerating.

The AI Acceleration: Adoption With No Barrier

AI is spreading faster than past technologies because the barriers are incredibly low:

- o   little or no money required
- o   generous free tiers
- o   cheap or free compute through cloud providers
- o   mature open-source libraries (transformers, diffusion, vector databases, model weights)
- o   worldwide accessibility
- o   no installation required
- o   instant usability

People can begin learning and experimenting with AI in seconds.

There has never been anything like this.

This unleashes enormous bottom-up pressure.

Employees are now:

- o   using AI at home before work
- o   writing smarter emails
- o   analyzing data
- o   brainstorming better ideas
- o   creating content
- o   building projects
- o   forming opinions and expectations

Individuals are becoming AI-augmented faster than organizations can govern them.

Governance Always Arrives Late — But This Time Consumers May Shape It

Traditionally, technology regulation is driven by:

- o big companies
- o industry lobbyists
- o legal teams
- o risk officers
- o political incentives

But the demand for policy — the pressure that forces lawmakers to act — always starts with ordinary people deciding what they expect from the tools they use every day.

Consumers create the need for regulation. But they rarely get a seat at the table.

As a result, policy is often shaped by the organizations with the most resources — companies that push for rules that protect their interests, not necessarily the public's. Unless consumer advocacy is strong, the final regulations tend to reflect industry priorities more than user needs.

But AI is different.

Because adoption is happening from the bottom up — individuals, students, creators, and employees using AI long before their institutions do — consumers have far more influence than they did during past technological shifts. Their expectations, habits, and demands are shaping the conversation before companies or governments can fully define it.

People are learning quickly. They're experiencing the benefits directly. They're becoming informed in a way the public rarely has during past tech revolutions.

Part of this book's purpose is to empower readers to:

o   see through hype

o   recognize misinformation

o   challenge unrealistic claims

o   and push back when something "AI-related" doesn't match reality

Informed consumers shape more than markets — they shape institutions, policy, and cultural norms.

When people understand how AI actually works, they become immune to fear-driven narratives and hype-fueled promises. Instead of reacting emotionally, they influence with:

o   practical facts

o   grounded expectations

o   and clarity

That influence reaches far beyond government.

It shows up when citizens respond thoughtfully to proposed regulations, question inflated corporate claims, or push back on political fear-mongering.

It shows up when communities demand accurate, honest descriptions of AI from leaders and media.

And increasingly, it shows up in local decision-making — school boards, libraries, parent groups, and civic organizations deciding what tools to adopt, how to protect students, what to allow, and what to avoid.

When people understand AI, they don't get swept up in moral panic or unrealistic fantasies.

They advocate with reality, not rhetoric.

They ask better questions.

They help institutions make choices based on evidence, not fear.

For the first time in a long time, the public can shape a major technological wave before the rules are written.

Organizations Must Adapt Their Governance to Their People — Not the Other Way Around

Real governance recognizes:

- o human behavior
- o organizational culture
- o risk tolerance
- o diverse use cases
- o and the fact that one size does not fit all

It must include:

- o appropriate controls
- o clear boundaries
- o ethical guidelines
- o defined risks
- o and the acknowledgment that employees are already experimenting

Businesses are made of people. And those people — their skills, knowledge, confidence, and curiosity — are what drive or stall AI adoption inside workplaces.

By the time a company writes its first AI policy, its employees have already been using AI privately for months — sometimes years. That's bottom-up adoption, not top-down strategy.

Cybersecurity evolved this way too. For years, companies treated security as a barrier.

Today, mature leaders understand that security, when framed correctly, is:

- o a competitive advantage
- o a trust signal
- o an enabler of better outcomes
- o a foundation of operational resilience

AI governance can follow the same trajectory.

Why This Matters for Business Leaders

Many leaders feel pressured to "adopt AI" because they're afraid of being left behind. But the truth is:

- o most don't understand what AI actually is
- o they rely on hype, marketing, or vendor promises
- o they make decisions without understanding the technology's behavior
- o their employees often know more than they do
- o they lack clarity on value, risk, or boundaries

A reader of this book will understand more practical AI behavior than many executives making multimillion-dollar decisions today.

This isn't an insult — it's an opportunity.

Organizations that empower informed employees will outpace those relying solely on top-down directives.

Consumers Can Shape AI's Future — Even When They Couldn't Shape the Past

Consumers didn't get a vote when call centers were outsourced. They didn't shape the terms of social media platforms. They didn't control the shift to online-only customer support. They didn't influence how companies offloaded responsibility to automated systems.

The results were mixed at best — often frustrating, sometimes harmful.

AI offers a rare opportunity:

Informed, curious, engaged consumers can shape the direction of AI use by demanding transparency, quality, and real value.

Companies will respond, because consumers now know enough to recognize when a system is serving them — versus serving the company.

This time, the public has leverage.

The Real Message

AI isn't just a business tool. It's not just a technology. It is a human capability amplifier.

Its evolution will be driven by:

- o   passionate individuals
- o   fringe adopters
- o   curious consumers
- o   researchers
- o   open-source communities
- o   and eventually, organizations trying to keep up

Understanding this pattern helps readers — and leaders — see beyond the hype and embrace AI as a partnership, not a threat.

And it equips them to help shape the future, rather than be shaped by it.

Chapter 18 — The Future We're Actually Building

And Why You're Going to Be Fine

By now, you've seen what AI is, what it isn't, how it behaves, what it can help with, and how to use it safely and creatively. You've seen its practical side, its humorous side, and the parts that feel human, even when they aren't. This final chapter looks forward — not through science fiction or fear, but through the same clear, grounded lens used throughout this book.

AI is the biggest technological shift since the internet, and possibly since electricity. And with every major shift, people experience the same emotions: curiosity, optimism, confusion, skepticism, excitement, and fear — especially fear about work, identity, and what the world will feel like for the next generation.

The reassuring truth is this: We've been here before. Many times.

The Pattern of Every Major Technological Shift

When cars replaced horses, people predicted:

o   widespread unemployment
o   chaos on the roads
o   broken supply chains
o   the collapse of small towns
o   moral decline due to "dangerous speeds"

Those fears weren't irrational. Jobs were lost. Entire industries did change. And yet new industries — larger and more complex — emerged in their place.

When word processors replaced typewriters, people worried that:

- o administrative roles would vanish
- o writing would become sloppy
- o errors would multiply
- o the value of professional documentation would plummet

Some of that disruption happened. But the ability to create, edit, and distribute written work exploded. Ideas became easier to express and share. New forms of communication emerged.

Film cameras were replaced by digital cameras. That transition also created fear — fear that photographic artistry would disappear, that digital images would feel disposable, and that professional photographers would lose their edge.

And yet digital imaging gave rise to the smartphone camera revolution, YouTube, photo editing, Instagram, Netflix, and an entire creator economy. Tens of millions of people now participate in storytelling and content creation who never would have had a platform in the film-only era.

Sometimes technologies come full circle. Vinyl returned. Film photography became trendy again. High-end mechanical watches and 1970s stereo receivers — once outdated — became more valuable than ever. Craftsmanship and nostalgia always find their place in a changing world.

Every transformation follows the same arc:

Short-term disruption.

Long-term expansion.

Individual pain.

Societal reinvention.

Fear.

Adaptation.

New opportunity.

AI will follow the same pattern.

And just like every past transformation, AI is already creating a wave of new infrastructure.

Cars needed roads, gas stations, traffic systems, repairs, and entire supply chains that didn't exist in the horse era. Word processors needed new software, new workflows, office training, digital publishing, and eventually the whole internet. Digital photography required sensors, storage, broadband, cloud platforms, and a global distribution network.

AI is no different.

Right now, we're in the early "infrastructure phase" — the part of the cycle where hundreds of billions of dollars flow into building the tools, models, chips, data pipelines, safety systems, and platforms that everything else will sit on.

In every technological wave, this investment comes first.

Over time, that spending shifts from building the infrastructure to operating it and inventing what runs on top of it. That is where entirely new roles, new industries, and new opportunities emerge — often in places no one predicted.

We don't feel the benefits immediately, because infrastructure comes before expansion. But expansion always follows.

The Job Question: Honest, Serious, Human

This is the question everyone thinks about:

"Will AI replace my job?"

The honest answer is:

AI will eliminate tasks, not people — but some jobs will shrink, some will disappear, and competition for the remaining roles will increase.

This deserves real acknowledgment, not optimism-as-distraction.

AI will automate repetitive, predictable, tightly defined tasks:

o   manual data entry
o   routine scheduling
o   standardized report drafting
o   form processing
o   basic coding
o   customer-service scripts
o   mechanical research tasks

Automation of tasks leads to pressure on roles. And before new roles emerge, job markets often compress. That compression creates more competition.

This isn't a failure of people — it's an unavoidable stage in every technological shift.

At the same time, AI will expand roles requiring:

o   judgment
o   ethics
o   empathy
o   communication
o   interpretation
o   creativity
o   leadership
o   hands-on practical skill
o   complex, cross-disciplinary thinking
o   the ability to orchestrate AI tools

This is where opportunity grows — but not all at once. New categories of jobs don't appear the moment automation arrives. Employers need time to:

o   understand new workflows
o   define new roles
o   write new job descriptions
o   learn what skills to hire for
o   size teams correctly

o   trust new processes

o   reorganize around new capabilities

Demand rises only after these organizational behaviors catch up.

This lag historically lasts years, not months. AI will be no different.

Who Is Most at Risk — And Why Multidimensional Experience Matters

The people at greatest risk are not the least intelligent or least capable. They are simply those whose jobs were built entirely around narrow, repeatable tasks.

Narrow roles are the first targets of automation because they have the least complexity to protect them.

What protects workers — now and in the future — is breadth.

People with experience across domains —

healthcare + operations,

teaching + counseling,

retail + logistics,

engineering + project management,

art + technology,

or any combination —

have an enormous advantage.

AI performs best when guided by someone who understands the problem space from multiple angles.

Cross-domain knowledge is a superpower. It helps you:

o   see patterns AI can't

o   ask better questions

o   judge whether answers make sense

o   translate between technical and practical worlds

o   coordinate across teams

o   spot missing pieces

o   understand context

o   guide AI toward outcomes that matter

People who know only one task are easiest to replace. People who know how things fit together are hardest.

The future belongs to the orchestrators.

You Don't Need to Become a Programmer — You Need to Learn How to Use AI

This idea is core to the entire book:

You don't need to learn how AI works under the hood. But you do need to learn how to use it.

You need to:

o   express ideas

o   break down problems

o   describe outcomes

o   ask for structure

o   evaluate responses

o   guide the tool

o   set boundaries

and, critically, ask:

"Teach me how to do this with AI."

AI can even teach you about AI. It can explain prompting, safety, hallucinations, model differences, ethics, and best practices in plain English.

You don't need prior expertise — the Scaffolding section of this book will include simple instructions, but AI itself can walk you through the rest.

In the future, the most valuable workers won't be those who write code. They'll be those who direct intelligence — both human and artificial — to achieve outcomes.

The Productivity Question: Will AI Give Us More Life?

This is an important concern worth addressing directly.

AI has the potential to free people from busywork and drudgery. But potential alone does not guarantee that organizations will use that freedom to create healthier work environments.

Many companies may choose to reduce staff or increase workload before they choose to shorten the workweek or reduce stress.

That's not an AI problem — it's a management philosophy problem.

AI will give companies productivity gains. What they do with those gains varies.

But here is the counterbalance:

When technology increases a worker's capability, the worker eventually gains leverage.

People who use AI effectively become:

- o   faster
- o   more capable
- o   more insightful
- o   more adaptable
- o   more creative
- o   more valuable
- o   more transferable
- o   and harder to replace

In the long run, workers who master these tools can negotiate differently, choose different paths, and move more freely across opportunities.

AI doesn't automatically give you more life — but it gives you the capacity to shape your life differently, to reduce the cognitive load of routine tasks, and to focus on the human parts of work that matter most.

Why the Future Will Be More Human, Not Less

As AI becomes more capable, the value of human traits becomes even clearer.

No dataset can recreate:

- compassion
- trust
- lived experience
- nuance
- ethics
- intuition
- courage
- personal connection
- the meaning behind a gesture or tone
- the wisdom gained from mistakes and recovery

These don't diminish in the AI era — they grow in importance.

The paradox of progress is that the more sophisticated our tools become, the more deeply we appreciate what only humans can do.

Fear FADES, Opportunity RISES

Every major technological shift begins with fear — not because people are weak, but because uncertainty is disorienting.

The worries you may feel right now are the same worries people felt during past revolutions in transportation, communication, industry, and computing.

But fear is not the destination.

Fear fades.

In this book, FADES isn't just a metaphor — it's the structure of your journey:

Fallacy, Anatomy, Doodles, Evolution, Scaffolding.

Five parts designed to dissolve confusion step by step.

As you moved through Fallacy and Anatomy, the strangeness of AI softened. Through Doodles and Evolution, understanding turned into capability and perspective. And with Scaffolding, you now have tools to carry that confidence forward.

Fear fades as understanding replaces confusion. It fades as complexity becomes clarity. It fades as you see what these tools can actually do — and what they can't.

And when fear fades, something else rises.

Opportunity rises.

RISE is the emotional progression unlocked by that journey:

READY — You now understand what AI is (and what it isn't).

INSPIRED — You've seen new possibilities open in front of you.

SEEKING — You're asking better questions and exploring ideas with intention.

EXPLORING — You're combining insight, skill, and curiosity to create something new.

This is the future you are stepping into — not one where AI replaces your humanity, but one where your humanity becomes the source of your advantage.

Fear FADES. Opportunity RISES. And you rise with it.

Where to Go From Here (A Call to Action)

You've reached the end of this book, but you've arrived at the beginning of something much larger.

You now understand what AI is, what it isn't, how it learns, how it helps, how it fails, and how it can make your life easier, safer, and more creative.

The world's knowledge is no longer locked away in books, classrooms, or experts' heads — or buried behind advertiser-influenced search results engineered to shape what you see instead of what you seek.

It's available to you instantly, the moment you become curious.

So here's the most meaningful next step:

Explore something — anything — that sparks your interest.

Pick a topic you've always wondered about:

astronomy,

cooking,

car maintenance,

sleep science,

economics,

woodworking,

interior design,

guitar chords,

the mating habits of squirrels — anything.

Ask AI to teach you the basics.

Revive an old passion by asking: "What has changed about ___ in the last ten or twenty years?"

Start a new hobby by asking: "How do I get into ___?"

You're not behind. You're not too late. You already have everything you need.

Experiment creatively, even if it feels silly.

Write a story with AI. Draft a poem. Design a perfect Saturday. Brainstorm a gift. Learn a hobby you never tried. Rediscover something you used to love.

Use AI the way an artist uses brushes — not to replace your imagination, but to reveal more of it.

AI can even teach you about AI:

prompting,

safety,

how to avoid misinformation,

how to build learning plans,

and how to use these tools responsibly.

Share what you learn.

Talk with your spouse, friends, children, or coworkers. Explain something AI helped you understand. Compare experiences.

If you've ever avoided participating in an online community because you felt nervous about your writing, let AI help you articulate your ideas clearly. The ideas are yours — AI just helps you express them.

Used thoughtfully, it becomes a bridge for sharing, not a machine for generating slop.

This is what it means for AI to liberate the world's knowledge. This is how it inspires creativity.

Not by replacing us — but by giving us new ways to think, learn, express ourselves, and connect with one another.

The world is changing, but you are far more ready for it than you realize.

Take one step. Ask one question. Let your curiosity lead the way.

The rest will follow — and the scaffolding that comes next will help you begin.

PART V — SCAFFOLDING (APPENDICES)

Tools, References, and Support to Help You Get Started

This is the S of FADES — Scaffolding. These final resources help you use AI responsibly, safely, and effectively in everyday life.

This section is designed for readers who want to dive in right away. If you're eager to start using AI — even before reading the full book — you can begin here. Each appendix gives you essentials in plain English: quick-start steps, practical guidance, and helpful references.

The main chapters offer depth, context, and stories. Part V gives you the tools to begin today.

It's called Scaffolding for a reason.

Scaffolding is temporary support — something you lean on while you build confidence, skill, and strength. After you've explored a bit and seen what AI can do, you won't need this structure in the same way. You'll move more freely, guided by your own understanding and experience.

Think of this section as the framework you can climb at your own pace — here when you need it, unnecessary once you've grown beyond it.

Appendix A — Your First 15 Minutes with AI

A simple, confidence-building quick start for absolute beginners.

You can learn AI in fifteen minutes — not by studying it, but by using it. This appendix gives you a simple, confidence-building path to get started.

You don't need to finish this book and then wonder, "Okay... now what?"

This appendix is your on-ramp — a small set of steps anyone can follow, even if you're not technical, even if you're a little nervous, even if you've never used an AI tool before.

No confusing jargon. No pressure. No prior knowledge needed.

Just fifteen minutes and a bit of curiosity.

Step 1 — Open ANY AI Tool (1 minute)

Choose whichever of these you already have:

- o ChatGPT (Web, iOS, or Android app)
- o Gemini (Web, Android, or iOS app)
- o Claude (Web or iOS app)
- o Perplexity (Web, iOS, or Android app)
- o Copilot (Web, Windows, or app)

It truly doesn't matter which one — they all work for this exercise.

Tip: If you're using ChatGPT or Gemini, the free version is fine. Paid versions are nice, but absolutely not required for learning.

Step 2 — Say This Out Loud in the Box (30 seconds)

Copy/paste this exact sentence:

"Hi! This is my first time. Explain how to use you in the simplest, friendliest way possible."

That's it.

Congratulations — you just prompted an AI.

Step 3 — Try Three Extremely Easy Things (5 minutes)

These three actions show you 80% of what AI can do.

Ask it to explain something you already know

Pick a topic you're comfortable with:

"Explain how cruise control works." "Explain what a deductible is in insurance." "Explain the difference between a muffin and a cupcake."

This builds trust because you can judge the answer.

Ask it to help with a real task

Try something tiny but useful:

"Rewrite this message to sound polite:" "Summarize this paragraph." "Help me draft a text to my friend."

Ask it to adapt the same idea three ways

This shows how flexible it can be:

"Now explain that like I'm 12." "Now explain it with a dog analogy." "Now explain it in two sentences."

You just learned prompt refinement — the real superpower.

Step 4 — Try a Safe Practice Question (3 minutes)

These reveal AI's strengths without risk:

"Explain something interesting about squirrels." "Tell me why sunsets are red." "Why does fresh bread go stale?"

Or something playful:

"Write a haiku about a goldendoodle who thinks she's in charge." "Tell me a calm, happy story about a cabin in the woods."

Zero risk. Pure learning.

Step 5 — Ask It to Teach You Something New (3 minutes)

This is the moment you start learning AI with AI.

Try one of these:

"Teach me one beginner concept about AI in plain English." "What's one thing a new AI user should know?" "Explain what a transformer model is without math." "What's the easiest way to avoid AI mistakes?"

Or:

"Explain to me how <anything you're interested in> works."

You're now learning the field — gently.

Step 6 — End With This Magic Prompt (1 minute)

This closes the loop and launches your future learning:

"Based on everything we've done, what should I try next?"

Make sure you type this in the same chat window you've been using — the AI can only build on the conversation if the context is still there.

This does three important things:

Shows the AI what pace you like

Adapts to your comfort level

Gives you a personalized next step

You now have a custom teacher that follows your lead.

Bonus: If You Want to Go Further

(You don't have to — but these unlock real fun.)

Try:

"Help me learn something I used to love but stopped doing."

"Help me pick a new hobby."

"Give me three ideas for how I can use AI tomorrow."

"Show me a mistake new users make, and how to avoid it."

Every time you ask a new question, AI becomes easier, safer, and more intuitive.

A Final Word for Beginners

If you can get through these fifteen minutes, you can use AI. If you can use AI, you can learn almost anything.

AI doesn't judge. AI doesn't get impatient. AI doesn't assume your background. AI adapts to your pace, style, and curiosity.

You're not learning AI. You're learning how to think with AI.

And that's the whole point.

Appendix B — A Practical Starter Guide to Using AI Tools

A friendly, simple way to begin — even if you've never used AI before

This appendix is one of the few product-specific sections of the book. Tools change fast — buttons move, features shift, capabilities improve, and names get updated. That's okay. The core skill of using AI always stays the same:

o   Ask a question
o   Give a task
o   Attach a photo or screenshot
o   Ask for clarification
o   Explore

If you can open a web browser or install an app on your phone, you're already capable of using AI.

You only need one AI tool to begin. You can try others anytime — your skills carry over.

Choosing an AI Tool (You Only Need One)

There are many widely used AI tools. You don't need all of them — just one that matches how you think, write, and work. Listed alphabetically are the most common options for beginners, with simple guidance on what each does best.

ChatGPT (OpenAI)

Use it in:

- o Browser: chatgpt.com
- o Mobile app: iPhone/Android

Great for:

- o everyday questions
- o recipes, planning, brainstorming
- o analyzing screenshots or documents
- o rewriting or improving content
- o troubleshooting and debugging
- o "explain this like I'm new" tasks
- o talking through ideas step by step

Why people like it: ChatGPT is the most balanced general-purpose AI — creative, helpful, and strong across a wide variety of tasks.

Claude (Anthropic)

Use it in:

- o Browser: claude.ai

Great for:

- o long-document support
- o deep reasoning
- o careful, nuanced writing
- o analyzing complicated material
- o structured thinking

Why people like it: Claude is the "thoughtful" model — excellent for people who want clarity, depth, and strong writing quality.

Gemini (Google)

Use it in:

- o Browser: gemini.google.com
- o Chrome sidebar
- o Android integration

Great for:

- search-like queries
- webpage summaries
- explaining confusing text
- practical, concise answers

Why people like it: Gemini feels fast, factual, and tightly integrated with Google search and Android tools.

Grok (xAI)

Access through: X Premium or Premium+ (with standalone web access rolling out) Browser: grok.com (may still require an X login)

Great for:

- humor and personality
- real-time web answers
- edgier, less-filtered responses
- Why people like it:
- It intentionally pushes the boundaries of tone and personality.
- It may offer responses other models avoid due to safer alignment settings.

Microsoft Copilot

Built into:

- Edge browser
- Windows 11
- Office apps (Word, Excel, PowerPoint, Outlook)

Great for:

- people who live inside Microsoft products
- drafting and editing in Office
- summarizing email
- working with spreadsheets

Why people like it: Copilot feels like an AI layer on top of the tools millions already use daily.

Which should you choose?

If you want the AI that's best at:

- o general purpose, creativity, writing → ChatGPT
- o search-like answers, quick lookups → Gemini
- o Office integration and productivity → Copilot
- o deep analysis, long documents, premium writing → Claude
- o humor, personality, fewer guardrails → Grok

There is no wrong choice. Start with whichever one you already have access to.

If you're unsure, simply ask any model:

"Compare ChatGPT, Gemini, Claude, Copilot, and Grok. Which is best for a beginner who wants ___ ?"

Free vs. Paid: What You Actually Need

At the time of publication, most people can use free tiers for everyday tasks — though this may evolve as the technology matures.

Free versions can handle:

- o summaries
- o everyday questions
- o analysis of screenshots and photos
- o hobby help
- o creative writing
- o basic planning
- o simple troubleshooting

Paid versions add:

- o stronger reasoning
- o longer documents
- o higher-quality images
- o voice features (varies by tool)
- o more powerful organizational tools
- o faster responses

Start free. Upgrade only if you hit a limit.

Privacy Basics (Simple but Important)

AI tools don't need personal details to work well. A few simple habits will keep you safe and comfortable.

What not to share

Avoid including:

- o Social Security numbers
- o credit card or bank info
- o passwords
- o medical records
- o private workplace data
- o anything you wouldn't share with a stranger

Why privacy controls matter

Even if companies don't "read" your chats in the traditional sense, your messages may:

- o appear in system logs
- o be temporarily stored for quality or safety checks
- o be reviewed by real humans to improve models
- o sit on servers with different security classifications

Caution is always smart.

Privacy settings to check

Most major tools include:

- o Chat history on/off
- o Memory on/off
- o Clear all conversations
- o Delete all data
- o Export your data
- o Limit training use of your prompts

Data retention policies differ — some delete immediately, others retain data for up to thirty days for operational needs.

If you're unsure, ask the AI:

"What is your data retention policy?"

"How do I delete all my data?"

"Do humans ever review my messages?"

Note: AI models sometimes hallucinate their own policies. For anything legal or privacy-related, always confirm by clicking the official Privacy or Help links on the website.

Simple rule: Treat AI like a friendly stranger — helpful, but don't over-share.

Using ChatGPT: Step-by-Step Basics

Browser version

Go to chat.openai.com and sign in.

App version

Download "ChatGPT" from the App Store or Google Play.

Your first message

Try something simple:

"Help me understand how to read my sleep pattern graph." "Write a friendly message to my neighbor about a branch that fell."

Attach a photo or screenshot

Tap the paperclip and attach:

- o an error message
- o a confusing form
- o a product label
- o a picture of a plant or bug

o   a photo of your dog doing something questionable

Then ask:

"What am I looking at?" "How do I fix this?" "Explain this in simple terms."

Try voice mode

On mobile, tap the microphone and talk naturally.

Try Projects (if available)

Projects help you:

o   organize research
o   keep templates
o   save ongoing topics

Using Gemini in Chrome

Access it through:

o   gemini.google.com
o   the Gemini button in Chrome
o   the Google app (mobile)

Summarize a webpage

While viewing any site:

"Summarize this page." "Explain this like I'm new to the topic."

Helpful everyday tasks

o   rewriting emails
o   understanding news articles
o   clarifying financial terms
o   helping with homework or learning

Using Microsoft Copilot

Where to find it

- o Edge sidebar
- o Windows 11
- o Word, Excel, Outlook (Copilot icon)

Helpful tasks

"Summarize this webpage." "Draft a reply to this email in a friendly tone." "Explain how this Excel formula works."

Text-to-Image Tools

Most AI tools generate images:

- o ChatGPT
- o Gemini
- o Copilot Designer
- o Canva

Try:

"Create a simple birthday card in watercolor style."

"Draw a golden retriever as a pirate."

"Make a minimalistic logo of a squirrel holding a coffee mug."

Voice Assistants

Voice mode is great for:

- o cooking help
- o driving questions
- o brainstorming
- o hands-free instructions
- o "talk through this with me" problems

ChatGPT, Gemini, and Copilot all offer voice options — primarily on their mobile apps.

Browser Integrations & Screenshots

A browser + AI is incredibly powerful.

AI can:

- o explain confusing news
- o read and summarize long pages
- o check websites for scam red flags
- o translate anything
- o clarify technical content

A very helpful use:

"Summarize this license agreement. Anything unusual? (I know you aren't a lawyer — just highlight anything that stands out.)"

Attach a screenshot or paste text — both work well.

Your First Week With AI

A simple, pressure-free way to get comfortable:

- o Day 1: Ask five simple questions
- o Day 2: Summarize an article
- o Day 3: Attach a screenshot
- o Day 4: Ask for help planning something
- o Day 5: Explore a hobby
- o Day 6: Try creative writing
- o Day 7: Try voice mode

Troubleshooting "Weird Answers"

AI sometimes responds with:

- o overconfidence
- o confusion
- o incomplete logic
- o mixed-up facts

When that happens, try:

"Give me your sources."

"Link me to a webpage with the same information."

"Explain your reasoning."

"Try again more simply."

"List three possibilities and tell me which is most likely."

"What additional information do you need from me?"

Most errors disappear with a clearer or narrower request.

Tools Change Fast — and That's Okay

New models appear every few months. Apps update. Buttons move. Features get renamed.

Don't worry.

The skill you're building — expressing what you need clearly — will always work, no matter what the interface looks like or which company makes the model.

AI is not about memorizing menus. It's about staying curious.

Appendix C — AI Concepts in Plain English

A friendly glossary for the curious

Introduction

This glossary explains common AI-related terms you may encounter as you explore beyond this book. Not every term here appears directly in the chapters — many are included because you'll see them in articles, news stories, videos, or conversations about AI.

You don't need to memorize anything.

If a word sparks your curiosity, ask AI:

"Explain ____ in simple terms, with examples."

"Explain ____ the way this book would explain it."

Think of this appendix as a friendly guide — a quick reference to help you feel confident, not a technical manual.

AI Terms (Alphabetical Glossary)

Agent / AI Agent An AI system that can take actions for you — booking a flight, checking email, summarizing documents, or managing tasks — not just answering questions.

AI (Artificial Intelligence) A computer system that performs tasks that normally require human thinking, such as understanding language, finding patterns, or making predictions.

AI Ethics / Ethical AI The principles and practices that ensure AI is used responsibly — focusing on fairness, safety, privacy, transparency, and reducing harm.

AI Governance The rules, processes, and oversight that ensure AI behaves responsibly and consistently.

AI Standards Guidelines created by industry or government that describe best practices for building safe, fair, transparent AI systems.

Alignment Teaching AI to behave safely, politely, and in line with human values.

API (Application Programming Interface) A tool that lets software connect to and use AI models behind the scenes.

Bias When AI unintentionally reflects unfair or skewed patterns from its training data.

Chatbot A conversational interface where you interact with AI using text or voice.

Closed Model An AI model whose inner workings are private. You can use it, but you can't see how it was trained.

Confidence Score A number representing how "sure" the AI is about an answer. High confidence doesn't always mean the answer is correct.

Context Window How much text an AI can consider at once. Larger windows allow longer conversations and bigger documents.

Controllability How easily a human can guide an AI's tone, structure, or behavior through prompts.

Data Governance How an organization manages data to ensure it's accurate, secure, private, and used appropriately.

Deterministic Output When the same input always produces the same answer. Some AI settings enforce this.

Embedding A way of turning words, sentences, or images into numbers so AI can compare meaning — like giving every idea a coordinate on a map.

Fine-Tuning Teaching an existing AI new skills or behaviors using additional examples.

Foundation Model A large pretrained AI model used as a base for many applications, from chatbots to analysis tools.

Fraud Detection Using AI to spot suspicious patterns that may indicate scams or account misuse.

Generative AI AI that creates new content — text, images, code, audio, or video.

Generalization An AI's ability to apply what it learned during training to new situations.

GPU (Graphics Processing Unit) A processor originally designed for graphics, now used to train and run AI because it performs thousands of operations in parallel.

Grounding Connecting AI answers to verified information — documents, PDFs, websites, or databases — instead of relying on guesses.

Guardrails Safety systems that prevent AI from producing harmful or dangerous content.

Hallucination When AI gives an answer that is incorrect but sounds confident — essentially, a guess presented as a fact.

Inference The process of an AI generating a response — its "thinking time."

Language Model A system trained to understand and generate human language.

Large Language Model (LLM) A very large language model trained on massive amounts of text to predict the next token and produce coherent responses.

Memory A feature that stores small user-provided details (preferences, facts, style). It isn't human memory — just notes the AI can reference later. When enabled, Memory becomes an extra data source for responses.

Model The "brain" of an AI system — the part that processes your input and generates answers.

Model Drift When an AI becomes less accurate over time because the world changes after training.

Model Version A new release of an AI model. Updates typically improve accuracy, safety, or capability.

Multimodal Model AI that understands or generates more than one type of input — text, images, audio, or video.

Neural Network A mathematical system inspired by how brains process information, helping AI learn patterns.

Open Source Model An AI model shared publicly so developers can run it, study it, or modify it — giving the community more control than fully closed models.

Parameter One of the millions (or billions) of internal values an AI adjusts during training.

Personalization When AI tailors responses to your interests, style, or preferences.

Physical AI / Robotics AI connected to machines that act in the real world — drones, robots, self-driving cars.

Plugin / Extension Add-ons that give AI extra abilities, like browsing or interacting with your calendar.

Probabilistic Output AI behavior where the same question may produce different answers because multiple responses are "likely."

Prompt The instructions or question you give to AI.

Prompt Engineering Crafting clear and structured instructions to get better results from AI.

RAG (Retrieval-Augmented Generation) A method where AI looks up information from documents or other sources you provide. It reduces hallucinations by grounding answers in additional data.

Reinforcement Learning A training method where AI learns from feedback like "good answer" or "bad answer."

Safety Layer Filters preventing harmful or dangerous outputs.

Synthetic Data Artificially created data used to train AI when real data is sensitive or unavailable.

Temperature A setting that controls how creative or predictable the AI is. Low = steady and factual. High = creative and surprising.

Token A small piece of a word — the building blocks AI uses to generate language.

Training The mathematical process where AI learns patterns from large amounts of data.

Training Data All the information AI was fed during training — books, websites, articles, code, conversations.

Transformer The architecture behind modern AI models, enabling fast and surprisingly effective language understanding.

Traditional Machine Learning Older forms of AI that learn patterns from structured data. Used for things like recommendations, spam filtering, credit scoring, and medical imaging.

Voice Cloning AI that can mimic a person's voice using audio samples.

Watermarking Invisible markers added to AI-generated content so it can be identified later.

Weight Another name for a parameter — the internal values AI adjusts to learn.

Appendix D — Types of AI and Where They Are Used

This book uses the term AI in the broad, everyday sense. Technically, though, many different kinds of AI exist. The focus of this book is Generative AI, because that's the technology people interact with most directly. But for readers who want the bigger picture — or simply want to use the right terms — it's helpful to understand the major categories of AI and where they show up in real life.

You do not need to memorize any of this. Just knowing these categories exist helps confusion fade.

Generative AI (Text, Images, Audio, Video)

What it is: AI that creates new content: text, images, audio, video, or combinations of all four.

How you encounter it in this book:

- o Large Language Models (LLMs) that help you write, learn, brainstorm, plan, summarize, analyze, and explore ideas.
- o Image and video generators that turn doodles into visuals and bring creativity to life.
- o Audio models that produce voices, soundtracks, or sound design.
- o Multimodal models that can analyze images, documents, slides, charts, and videos — and generate new ones.

Examples: ChatGPT, Claude, Gemini, Midjourney, DALL·E, Runway, Sora.

Where it shows up in daily life:

- o writing assistance and documentation
- o customer support chatbots
- o marketing content
- o homework and study help
- o code generation
- o research summaries
- o video scripting and editing
- o social media content creation

Impact on work: Generative AI dramatically increases individual productivity. A task that once took eight hours may now take one.

Companies can use that capability to:

- o increase output with the same number of people, or
- o reduce the number of people needed for the same output

The technology doesn't choose. Management does.

Agentic AI (AI Agents)

What it is: Generative AI that doesn't just respond — it can take action. Agents use LLMs as the "brain" and add the ability to:

- o perform tasks
- o interact with tools
- o repeat steps
- o plan
- o reason across long sequences
- o pursue goals

Examples:

- o email-reading and reply-drafting agents
- o research agents that gather, summarize, and compare information

- o workflow automation agents
- o project assistants that track tasks or prepare materials
- o customer service agents that resolve cases end-to-end

Where it shows up today:

- o personal assistants
- o business process automation
- o software engineering copilots
- o research automation
- o task orchestration tools

Impact on work: Agentic AI shifts work from doing the task to reviewing, directing, and improving work done by AI.

It changes the shape of jobs more than it eliminates them.

Predictive AI (Machine Learning)

What it is: AI that analyzes historical data to predict future outcomes or classify information. It doesn't create new content — it calculates probability.

Examples:

- o Netflix-style recommendations
- o Spam filtering
- o Credit scoring
- o Fraud detection
- o Supply-chain forecasting

Where it shows up: Everywhere — usually invisibly. Traditional ML powers nearly every modern digital system.

Impact on work: Predictive systems automate analysis, accelerate decision-making, and reduce error in data-heavy workflows.

Traditional ML gives organizations superpowers in:

- o forecasting

o logistics
o fraud detection
o clinical insights
o scientific research
o risk modeling

Generative AI didn't replace traditional ML — it expanded the toolbox.

Computer Vision (AI That "Sees")

What it is: AI that analyzes images and video. It detects objects, recognizes faces, reads handwriting, and interprets medical scans.

Examples:

o Photo sorting in your phone
o Self-driving car cameras
o Security systems
o Medical imaging and diagnostics

Where it appears in generative AI: Any time you upload a picture, diagram, slide deck, or PDF and the AI interprets it — that's computer vision working with generative AI.

Impact on work: Transforms any task requiring visual interpretation — from quality control to radiology. Computer vision automates tasks that once required human eyes:

o inspection
o sorting
o monitoring
o reading documents
o analyzing medical scans

Workers shift toward oversight and interpretation rather than manual review.

Robotics & Physical AI

What it is: AI connected to machines that move, navigate, sense, or manipulate the physical world.

Examples:

- o   warehouse robots
- o   drone delivery
- o   self-driving cars
- o   surgical robots
- o   consumer robots (vacuums, mowers, household assistants)

Impact on work: Robotics blends physical labor with digital intelligence.

Most roles evolve into human + robot teamwork, focusing on:

- o   oversight
- o   coordination
- o   troubleshooting
- o   maintenance
- o   higher-level decision-making

Expert Systems (Rules-Based AI)

What it is: Older AI that follows logic trees and fixed rules. No learning — it applies programmed knowledge.

Examples:

- o   Legacy banking approval systems
- o   Fraud rules engines
- o   Tax preparation logic systems

Impact on work: These systems automate predictable tasks and free humans for:

- o   nuance
- o   judgment
- o   empathy

o   exception handling

They still power a huge portion of enterprise operations today.

Putting It All Together

Most people experience AI through generative models because they feel conversational, creative, and helpful. But behind the scenes, the AI ecosystem is much broader:

o   Traditional ML predicts and classifies.
o   Vision models interpret images and video.
o   Robotics interacts with the physical world.
o   Agents take action.
o   Generative AI creates.

The future of AI is the fusion of these systems — tools that can see, think, act, and create within a single workflow.

And the best part?

You don't need deep technical knowledge to benefit. You just need enough clarity to let fear fade and curiosity rise.

Appendix E — A Short History of AI That Won't Put You to Sleep

A fun, fast tour through seventy years of breakthroughs, flops, surprises, and accidental inventions that led to the AI you're using today.

Why This History Matters

AI history isn't just a list of dates — it's a decades-long adventure full of big ideas, wrong turns, bold predictions, collapses, recoveries, and the occasional moment when video-game hardware accidentally changed the world.

You only need the highlights. And whenever you want more, just ask an AI:

"Tell me more about this moment in AI history."

"Explain this like I'm 12."

"Who were the key people involved?"

AI is now the best teacher of its own history.

Long Before Computers: Humans Imagined Smart Machines

Humans have always dreamed of creating intelligence:

- o   Greek mythology imagined Talos, a giant bronze robot guardian.

o   Early inventors built automata — mechanical birds, musical boxes, and clockwork figures.

o   Mary Shelley wrote *Frankenstein* in 1818, reflecting fear of human-made intelligence.

o   Mathematicians developed the foundations: Boolean logic, probability, and rules for reasoning.

Try asking AI: "Show me three ancient myths about artificial beings." "How did *Frankenstein* influence AI ethics?"

The 1950s: "Can Machines Think?"

This is where modern AI truly begins.

Alan Turing

Turing asked the question that still echoes today:

"Can machines think?"

His famous Turing Test was a playful way of asking: If you can't tell whether you're talking to a machine or a person, does it matter?

Early AI Experiments

Programs played tic-tac-toe, checkers, and solved small logic puzzles.

IBM Mainframes Arrive

The IBM 701 launched in 1952. By the early 1960s:

o   large businesses
o   universities
o   and the IRS

were using mainframes for tasks like payroll, census processing, and tax calculations.

These systems used structured rules — the early roots of logic-based intelligence.

Try asking AI: "Explain what IBM mainframes could do in the 1950s."

The 1960s–1970s: Symbolic AI, LISP, and the First AI Winter

Researchers believed intelligence came from rules and logic.

Symbolic AI

The idea was simple and seductive:

If we teach the computer enough rules, it will behave intelligently.

LISP — The AI Language

Created in 1958 by John McCarthy, LISP became the language of AI research at MIT, Stanford, and many others.

It's still used today in:

o   advanced robotics
o   academic research
o   symbolic reasoning systems

Famous Systems

o   ELIZA — the "therapist" chatbot that made people feel surprisingly understood
o   SHRDLU — a system that understood English, but only in a world of blocks

Sci-Fi Shapes Expectations

o   *Star Trek*'s conversational computer
o   HAL 9000 from *2001: A Space Odyssey* — intelligent, eerie, and unsettlingly calm

The First AI Winter

Optimism collapsed when researchers realized that intelligence is not just a giant list of IF–THEN rules.

Systems broke the moment reality became unpredictable.

Funding dried up, public excitement faded, and progress stalled.

This multi-year downturn became known as the *first AI winter* — the earliest of several periods of reduced investment, momentum, and belief.

Try asking AI: "Explain symbolic AI using a cooking analogy."

The 1980s: Expert Systems — When AI Became a Bureaucrat

AI reinvented itself as rule-based corporate assistants.

Expert systems powered:

- o early medical diagnosis
- o financial modeling
- o credit assessments
- o industrial scheduling
- o insurance underwriting

They ran on LISP machines, specialized computers built just to execute LISP efficiently.

The problem?

They were extremely smart until something unexpected happened.

Like a bureaucrat who can fill out any form perfectly — as long as the form never changes.

Meanwhile, hardware improved dramatically: faster microprocessors and workstations became common.

The 1990s: Machine Learning Quietly Takes Over

AI shifted from rules to learning from examples.

- o Spam filters learned from emails.
- o Search engines became smarter.
- o Early recommendation systems appeared.
- o Speech recognition improved.

o   Banks adopted machine learning for fraud detection.

People didn't call this "AI," but it was — quietly powering much of the growing internet.

Cultural AI moment: *The Matrix* (1999) captured society's fascination — and fear — of machine intelligence.

Try asking AI: "Show me how early recommendation systems worked."

The 2000s: Big Data + GPUs = The Perfect Storm

Two revolutions collided.

Big Data

The internet produced oceans of text, images, clicks, and logs — perfect training fuel.

GPUs (Graphics Processing Units)

Originally designed for video games.

Gamers demanded:

o   better lighting
o   smoother animation
o   realistic shadows
o   explosions, reflections, water physics

So companies built GPUs that could process massive amounts of visual math.

Researchers realized:

The math used to render a dragon in a video game is similar to the math needed to train a neural network.

The GPU became the engine of modern AI.

A single high-end gaming GPU has more parallel processing power than entire 1960s supercomputer facilities.

Try asking AI: "Explain why GPUs made deep learning possible."

2012: Deep Learning Bursts Through the Door

A model called AlexNet crushed the global image-recognition competition.

It ran on GPUs and proved:

- o neural networks can outperform traditional algorithms
- o computers can learn complex patterns
- o hardware finally caught up with imagination

Tech companies pivoted almost overnight.

2017–2020: Transformers — The Architecture That Changes Everything

In 2017, researchers introduced the Transformer architecture:

- o reads text in parallel
- o remembers context across long passages
- o scales effortlessly with more data
- o understands word relationships better than anything before it

GPT Explained

GPT stands for:

- o G — Generative
- o P — Pre-trained
- o T — Transformer

Transformers made modern AI possible.

2022: ChatGPT — The Day AI Became Mainstream

On November 30, 2022, ChatGPT launched — and everything changed.

For the first time, an AI model:

- o felt helpful
- o felt conversational
- o felt accessible
- o felt usable by everyone

It was the interface — the friendly chat window — that unleashed AI on the world.

Ask ChatGPT: "Explain why your launch changed everything." (It will give a surprisingly humble answer.)

2023–2025: The Acceleration Era

Suddenly every major tech company had a model:

- o GPT-4
- o Claude 3
- o Gemini Ultra
- o Llama 3 (and beyond)
- o Mixtral
- o Dozens of open-source variants

Here's the twist:

They're all built on the same Transformer blueprint.

Different training data. Different strengths. Same architecture.

Capabilities exploded:

- o AI-generated images
- o AI-generated video
- o AI-generated voices
- o multimodal reasoning
- o chart and document interpretation

- o AI agents that take actions
- o entire models running on laptops — even phones

Hardware surged too:

- o massive GPU clusters
- o AI-optimized processors
- o cloud supercomputers
- o powerful local models for consumer devices

Try asking AI: "Summarize the major AI models released between 2023 and 2025."

2026 and Beyond: What Happens Next?

A realistic, optimistic, grounded look.

Nobody knows exactly what comes next — but decades of patterns point to several likely trends.

AI becomes boring — in the best possible way

It shifts from "impressive new technology" to everyday infrastructure, like:

- o spreadsheets
- o GPS
- o smartphones
- o the internet

Most AI use will happen quietly in the background.

Businesses reorganize around AI

Leaders finally understand:

AI doesn't replace jobs — it replaces tasks.

Organizations will restructure accordingly:

- o new hybrid roles
- o new job categories
- o fewer repetitive tasks

o   more emphasis on creativity, judgment, oversight

Some scary incidents will happen

Every major technology has growing pains:

o   email → phishing
o   cars → accidents
o   the internet → misinformation

AI will have misuses, too — but society adapts, always.

Big scientific breakthroughs

Expect acceleration in:

o   medicine
o   materials science
o   genetics
o   drug discovery
o   robotics
o   accessibility tools

AI becomes a core engine of scientific progress.

Everyday people become dramatically more capable

AI becomes:

o   teacher
o   research partner
o   project advisor
o   creative collaborator
o   translator
o   planner

It won't replace human creativity — it will multiply it.

Try asking AI: "Show me realistic predictions for the next five years of AI."

What You Should Take Away

AI did not appear suddenly. It rests on seventy-plus years of research, trial and error, imagination, and persistence.

Modern breakthroughs are built on:

- o   symbolic logic
- o   machine learning
- o   neural networks
- o   deep learning
- o   transformers
- o   and yes — gaming hardware

The "magic" is engineering, math, and scale.

Understanding the past makes the future less intimidating and more exciting.

And now, whenever you're curious, you can simply ask:

"Teach me more about this part of your history."

AI will happily take it from here.

Appendix F — Additional Reading

Curated for the curious reader who wants to go deeper — without needing a computer science degree.

This is not a traditional bibliography stuffed with academic formatting and tiny print. It's a guided list of books, reports, papers, and ideas that shaped modern AI, along with simple prompts you can use to explore any source with the help of AI.

You do not need to read everything here. Think of this appendix like a menu: browse, skim, sample, and follow your curiosity.

Whenever something interests you, ask your AI assistant:

"Summarize this book." "Explain the key ideas in plain English." "Give me a beginner-friendly version." "Find related sources or newer updates."

AI is now the friendliest librarian on earth.

Books for General Readers (No Technical Background Needed)

These books tell stories, not equations. They're great starting points for anyone new to AI or big ideas.

Life 3.0 — Max Tegmark

A guided tour of possible AI futures — optimistic, cautious, and curious.

The Alignment Problem — Brian Christian

A beautifully human account of the struggle to make AI behave as intended.

Genius Makers — Cade Metz

Journalistic storytelling about the people who built modern AI.

The Master Algorithm — Pedro Domingos

A high-level explanation of the five "tribes" of machine learning.

Superintelligence — Nick Bostrom

Influential book exploring long-term risk scenarios (read with balance).

Thinking, Fast and Slow — Daniel Kahneman

Not about AI, but essential for understanding human reasoning and bias.

Try asking AI:

"Give me five takeaways from *Genius Makers*."

"What does *Life 3.0* say about how AI might evolve?"

"Which of these is best for someone just getting started?"

Industry Reports (Readable, Visual, and Practical)

Think of these as "state of the union" updates for the AI world. They're surprisingly accessible.

Stanford AI Index Report (annual)—The most comprehensive overview of global AI progress, performance, and adoption.

McKinsey State of AI (annual)—Business trends, ROI, and economic effects.

Deloitte AI Adoption Studies—Clear breakdowns of how companies adopt and struggle with AI.

OpenAI System Cards & Technical Overviews—High -level explanations of how GPT-based models work.

Google DeepMind Research Blog—Breakthroughs and research explained for humans, not engineers.

OECD AI Policy Observatory—Global perspective on AI governance and ethics.

Try asking AI:

"Summarize the key findings from the latest Stanford AI Index."

"What do McKinsey and Deloitte disagree on?"

"Explain this chart from the AI Index in plain English."

Government & International Studies

These documents explain how nations think about safety, policy, and regulation.

NIST AI Risk Management Framework (U.S.)

The most practical guide for businesses trying to use AI safely.

EU AI Act (summaries available)

A comprehensive regulatory framework the world is watching closely.

White House Blueprint for an AI Bill of Rights

Focused on discrimination, privacy, and fairness.

UK AI Safety Institute Reports

Technical evaluations of cutting-edge models.

UNESCO Recommendations on AI Ethics

A global consensus statement about values and rights.

Try asking AI:

"Explain the EU AI Act like I'm a high-school student."

"What are the main components of the NIST AI Risk Framework?"

"How might the AI Bill of Rights affect everyday users?"

Foundational Research Papers

You do not need to read these — but you can explore them with AI summaries. These papers shaped everything your AI assistant does today.

Alan Turing — "Computing Machinery and Intelligence" (1950)

Introduced the idea of machines "thinking" and proposed the Turing Test.

Dartmouth AI Conference Proposal (1955)

The moment AI became its own field.

Rumelhart, Hinton & Williams — Backpropagation (1986)

The algorithm that lets neural networks learn by adjusting weights.

Hochreiter & Schmidhuber — LSTM (1997)

Breakthrough for handling long sequences like speech or text.

LeCun et al. — Convolutional Networks (1998)

Foundation of modern computer vision.

Goodfellow et al. — Generative Adversarial Networks (2014)

Where realistic synthetic imagery began.

Vaswani et al. — "Attention Is All You Need" (2017)

Introduced the Transformer — the architecture behind GPT, Claude, Gemini, and nearly every modern AI system.

Try asking AI:

"Summarize 'Attention Is All You Need' without math."

"Why did Transformers replace older approaches like RNNs?"

"Explain GANs using a cooking analogy."

Safety, Ethics, and Governance

Balanced resources for understanding the challenges and responsibilities of AI.

Anthropic — Constitutional AI Research

A framework for making AI behavior more consistent and principled.

OpenAI Safety & Preparedness Reports

Readable explanations of how large models are evaluated and tuned.

Center for Humane Technology Digital well-being and societal impact.

Future of Humanity Institute Ethics, long-term risk, and governance.

Harvard Berkman Klein Center Technology, law, rights, and society.

Try asking AI:

"What is Constitutional AI, and why does it matter?"

"Explain major AI safety concerns in non-scary terms."

"Compare OpenAI's and Anthropic's safety approaches."

History of Computing & Technology

These books explain how technologies evolve — helpful context for understanding AI's acceleration.

The Innovators — Walter Isaacson

How the digital revolution began.

Hackers — Steven Levy

Cultures and communities that shaped early computing.

Dealers of Lightning — Michael Hiltzik

The legendary Xerox PARC labs that invented the future.

Where Wizards Stay Up Late — Hafner & Lyon

The story of how the internet was built.

The Soul of a New Machine — Tracy Kidder

A gripping inside look at early hardware engineering.

Try asking AI:

"What lessons from *Dealers of Lightning* apply to modern AI startups?"

"How did early computing culture shape today's tech world?"

Parallel Transformations

The Best Historical Mirrors of Today's AI Shift

These books are enormously helpful for understanding what's happening today — because society has undergone transformations like this before.

A Nation of Steel — Thomas Misa

How steel reshaped America's infrastructure, industries, and workforce.

Railroaded — Richard White

How railroads unleashed economic growth, chaos, fraud, innovation, and new national systems.

The Visible Hand — Alfred Chandler

How modern corporations (and management) evolved due to new technologies.

Steel: From Mine to Mill — Brooke Stoddard

A walk through the rise of mass manufacturing.

Drive: The Definitive History of Motoring

How the automobile revolution changed cities, mobility, work, and culture.

The Machine That Changed the World — Womack, Jones, Roos

The Toyota Production System — lean, efficient, adaptive.

Rivethead — Ben Hamper

A raw account of factory life during industrial transition.

Empires of Light — Jill Jonnes

The electrification of America — hype, resistance, fear, and transformation.

The Victorian Internet — Tom Standage

The telegraph era — the first communication revolution: hype cycles, scams, and global connectivity.

Try asking AI:

"Compare the rise of the railroad to the rise of AI."

"What parallels exist between electrification and AI adoption?"

"Summarize *A Nation of Steel* and connect it to the AI workforce shift."

Popular Science & Big-Idea Reading

Books that explore intelligence, complexity, and the nature of information itself.

Gödel, Escher, Bach — Douglas Hofstadter

A playful but profound look at patterns, meaning, and thought.

The Information — James Gleick

The history of information theory — the backbone of computing.

Sapiens — Yuval Noah Harari

How human cognition evolved and how we create shared meaning.

The Singularity Is Near — Ray Kurzweil

A futurist vision of accelerating technology.

Try asking AI: "Explain the central metaphor in *Gödel, Escher, Bach*."
"How does *Sapiens* relate to artificial intelligence?"

Fiction That Shaped How We Imagine AI

These stories influenced culture long before real AI existed — and many ideas still shape expectations today.

2001: A Space Odyssey — Arthur C. Clarke

HAL 9000 — calm, eerie intelligence with human flaws.

I, Robot — Isaac Asimov

The classic Three Laws of Robotics.

Do Androids Dream of Electric Sheep? — Philip K. Dick

The emotional side of artificial beings.

Neuromancer — William Gibson

Cyberpunk origins of today's internet culture.

The Moon Is a Harsh Mistress — Robert Heinlein

A friendly, self-aware computer that might be closer to reality than we once imagined.

The Three-Body Problem — Cixin Liu

Complex, imaginative, and full of mind-bending science.

Try asking AI: "Summarize Asimov's Three Laws."

"How is HAL different from modern AI models?"

"Compare the AI themes in *Neuromancer* with today's technologies."

Final Encouragement

This appendix is not homework.

Let yourself explore at your own pace. Follow what interests you. Skip the rest.

And remember:

AI can help you learn about AI — and everything else.

You now have everything you need to continue the journey.

www.ingramcontent.com/pod-product-compliance
Lightning Source LLC
Chambersburg PA
CBHW021920190326

41519CB00009B/864